ENDANGERED SPEECHES

HOW THE ACLU, IRS & LBJ THREATEN EXTINCTION OF FREE SPEECH

William J. Federer

D1292614

ENDANGERED SPEECHES

HOW THE ACLU, IRS & LBJ THREATEN EXTINCTION OF FREE SPEECH

William J. Federer

ENDANGERED SPEECHES
- HOW THE ACLU, IRS & LBJ
THREATEN EXTINCTION OF FREE SPEECH
by William J. Federer

To duplicate larger portions, please contact: wjfederer@aol.com, P.O. Box 4363, St. Louis, MO 63123, 314-487-4395, 314-487-4489 fax, www.amerisearch.net 1-888-USA-WORD voice/fax

HISTORY / EDUCATION   ISBN   0-9778085-8-0

Special acknowledgement to Vision America's Rick Scarborough, described by CNN's Christiane Amanpur as "one of God's Warriors," as this book was born out of research for a series of meetings he arranged with pastors in New Mexico.
And to former NFL Chicago Bears & OSU football star, Pastor Paul Blair, who challenges pastors to get in the game!
And to the pastors of the Alliance Defense Fund's Pulpit Initiative.

As owner of this book, you are entitled to a limited-time offer to receive a free *ebook* of this title by visiting www.AmericanMinute.com Click "Contact" and send an email with the subject line SEND FREE EBOOK offer "Endangered Speeches." Permission is granted to forward the ebook via email.

Amerisearch, Inc., P.O. Box 20163, St. Louis, MO 63123
1-888-USA-WORD, 314-487-4395 voice/fax
www.amerisearch.net, wjfederer@gmail.com

The Church is...
the conscience of the state.

-MLK, Jr.

TABLE
OF
CONTENTS

George Washington
First President
United States of America

RELIGION & POLITICS

"If I could have entertained the slightest apprehension that the Constitution framed by the Convention, where I had the honor to preside, might possibly endanger the religious rights of any ecclesiastical Society, certainly I would never have placed my signature to it."
- George Washington, May 10, 1789, to United Baptist Churches of Virginia

Historically, churches in America had freedom to speak on political issues, as many colonies were founded by pastors with their congregations holding government meetings in the church.

Churches were not only exempt from taxes, but many colonies and early State governments actually collected taxes to support churches.

Dr. Rev. Martin Luther King, Jr.
Pastor, civil rights activist
Ebeneezer Baptist Church, Atlanta, Georgia

Churches were valued by government:

First, for maintaining a virtuous, responsible populace, as the more internal moral laws citizens had, the less external laws they needed;

Secondly, for providing charitable social services, such as: hospitals, orphanages, schools, education, feeding the poor, benevolence, welfare ministries, caring for maimed soldiers, immigrants, prisoners, unwed mothers, widows, shut-ins, homeless and juvenile delinquents.

The tradition of exemption from taxes for charitable services can be traced back to the British Statute of Charitable Uses of 1601.

In addition to moral and social concerns, American pastors felt a biblical responsibility to be the conscience of society, speaking out on public issues.

Dr. Rev. Martin Luther King, Jr., Pastor of Ebeneezer Baptist Church, Atlanta, George, stated in his sermon, Strength to Love, 1963:

The Church must be reminded that it is not the master or the servant of the state, but rather the conscience of the state.
It must be the guide and the critic of the state, and never its tool.

John Leland
Baptist Pastor, Virginia and Massachusetts
Supported Thomas Jefferson and James Madison

Henry Ward Beecher
Pastor, abolitionist,
Plymouth Congregational Church, Brooklyn, NY

If the church does not recapture its prophetic zeal, it will become an irrelevant social club without moral or spiritual authority.

During the Revolutionary War, patriotic pastors who spoke out against King George III were referred to as the "black regiment," as traditional clerical robes were black.

Baptist preacher **John Leland**, along with Presbyterian and Methodist pastors, openly encouraged church members to support the elections of Thomas Jefferson and James Madison, as they promised to disestablish Virginia's established Church of England, which had persecuted and imprisoned Baptists prior to the Revolutionary War.

An 18th century tradition was for pastors to deliver "Election Day Sermons" telling their congregations how to vote in light of Scripture.

Prior to the Civil War, notable pastors spoke out against slavery, such as

Henry Ward Beecher of the Plymouth Congregational Church, Brooklyn, NY; **Elijah Lovejoy** of the Presbyterian Church, St. Louis, MO; **Charles Finney** of the Brooklyn Tabernacle, Manhattan, NY; and **John Parkman** of the First Unitarian Church, Dover, NH.

Archbishop John Baptist Purcell
Cincinnati, Ohio,
stood against slavery.

During the Civil War, Cincinnati's Catholic Archbishop, **John Baptist Purcell**, took much criticism for standing against slavery, even when a mob threatened to destroy the cathedral. Years later, President Rutherford B. Hayes noted in his diary after speaking to the Catholic Knights of America in Fremont, Ohio, September 9, 1890:

> Archbishop Purcell strung the American flag, in the crisis of our fate, from the top of the Cathedral in Cincinnati, April 16, 1861! The spire was beautiful before, but the Catholic prelate made it radiant with hope and glory for our country!

Churches did not always speak out, but it was up to each individual pastor to make that decision.

Many took stands regarding women suffrage, child labor, prohibition of alcohol, unions, war, immigration, civil rights, Sabbath observance, as well as lobbying Federal and State Governments to adopt holidays such as Mothers' Day and Fathers Day.

Churches did not have to worry about losing their IRS tax-exempt status because prior to 1913, there was no IRS and no IRS Tax Code.

Melville W. Fuller
Supreme Court Chief Justice,
nominated by President Grover Cleveland

IRS
&
TAX-EXEMPT
STATUS

"The original expectation **was that the power of direct taxation would be exercised only in extraordinary exigencies."**
- Justice Melville W. Fuller, 1895, *Pollack v Farmers Loan & Trust*

Lincoln had an emergency, temporary Income Tax to raise $750 million to finance the Civil War, but it was repealed in 1873.

This tax did not infringe on the rights of pastors and churches to speak their views, as they understood the First Amendment to limit "Congress," not churches.

In 1894, the Federal Government attempted to pass the first "peace time" Income Tax with its Tariff Act.

Stephen Johnson Field
Supreme Court Justice,
nominated by Abraham Lincoln

The Supreme Court struck it down, declaring Income Tax unconstitutional in the 1895 case of *Pollack v Farmers Loan & Trust.*

Justice Stephen J. Field wrote:

> The **income tax law** under consideration...discriminates between those who receive an income of four thousand dollars and those who do not...[It] is class legislation.
> Whenever a distinction is made in the burdens a law imposes or in the benefits it confers on any citizens by reason of their birth, or wealth, or religion, it is **class legislation,** and **leads inevitably to oppression and abuses...**
> The objectional legislation...is the same in essential character as that of the English income statute of 1691, which taxed Protestants at a certain rate, Catholics, as a class, at double the rate of Protestants, and Jews at another and separate rate.

Since the proposed 1894 Tariff Act was to have placed a 2 percent Income Tax on "for-profit" corporations, it necessitated the government coming up with a category for "not-for-profit" corporations.

Woodrow Wilson
28th President
United States of America

This category, the forerunner of "501(c)3," stated in Section 32 of the 1894 Tariff Act:

Nothing herein contained shall apply to corporations, companies or associations organized and conducted solely for charitable, religious or educational purposes.

In 1913, Democrat President Woodrow Wilson finally pushed through the 16th Amendment and the Internal Revenue Service was born.

Federal Laws are compiled in the United States Code, categorized under 50 Titles. Title 26 contains the Federal Tax Laws and is referred to as the "IRS Code," enforced by the U.S. Treasury Department.

The IRS Code's 501(c)3 category was originally just for charitable, religious and educational foundations: 1) **exempting them from paying taxes**; and 2) **allowing tax deductions for contributors.**

The 501(c)3 category grew to include:

Corporations, and any community chest fund (added 1921), or foundation, organized and operated exclusively for religious, charitable, scientific (added 1913), testing for public

United States Treasury
Washington, D.C.

safety (added 1954), literacy (added 1921) or educational purposes, or to foster national or international amateur sports competition (added 1976) or for the prevention of cruelty to children or animals (added 1918).

Many find it an odd that churches are in the same IRS category as foundations to foster amateur sports competitions and foundations to prevent cruelty to animals.

Wealthy individuals, such as Andrew Carnegie, John D. Rockefeller and Henry Ford used the 501(c)3 category to create foundations into which they could transfer assets to avoid taxes, yet still direct the use of their funds.

The government then imposed more restrictions on 501(c)3 foundations, finally separating private foundations from public charities in 1964.

After Russia's Bolshevik Revolution in 1917, Communist agitators spread to other countries, including the United States.

Soon Communists were pamphleteering, working as community organizers and recruiting in labor unions. To stop them, Congress passed the Espionage Act of 1917 and Sedition Act of 1918. In 1919, the Communist Party USA was founded.

Al Smith
Governor of New York
Presidential Candidate

In 1919, the U.S. Treasury Department argued that foundations "formed to disseminate controversial or partisan propaganda" could not be considered "educational" 501(c)3 foundations.

In 1920, a World War I draft-dodger named Roger Baldwin with socialist and communist anti-war protesters, founded the ACLU 501(c)3 Foundation to defend those accused of disloyal activities. Viewed as leftist, the nation has since moved to the left, so its relative perception has modified.

In 1923, Roger Baldwin's friend, Margaret Sanger, founded a 501(c)3 organization that became Planned Parenthood, supported by the Rockefeller and Carnegie Foundations.

Churches still spoke out politically, as seen in the 1928 Presidential Election where many Protestant churches opposed Governor Al Smith of New York, who was campaigning to become the nation's first Catholic President.

In the 1934 Revenue Act, Congress further restricted 501(c)3 foundations from influencing legislation by "substantial" lobbying, though the term "substantial" was not defined.

Though most churches were not "corporations" for religious purposes, the IRS began to treat them as if they had incorporated.

Pastors and churches still had the freedom to support candidates until things changed in 1954.

Lyndon Baines Johnson
36th President
Vice-President 1960-1963
U.S. Senator from Texas 1949-1960

LBJ'S AMENDMENT

*"**D**enying tax-exempt status to not only those people who influence legislation but also to those who intervene in any political campaign on behalf of any candidate for any public office."*
- Senator Lyndon Baines Johnson, July 2, 1954

In 1954, Senator Lyndon Baines Johnson of Texas proposed an amendment to the IRS Tax Code.

The Congressional Record, July 2, 1954, (9604; New York Times, July 3, 1954) reported:

Mr. JOHNSON of Texas. Mr. President, **I have an amendment** at the desk, which I should like to have stated.

Lyndon Baines Johnson

The PRESIDING OFFICER. **The Secretary will state the amendment.** The Chief Clerk.

On page 117 of the House Bill, in **section 501(c)3,** it is proposed to strike out "individuals, and" and insert "individual," and strike out "influence legislation," **and insert "influence legislation, and which does not participate in, or intervene in (including the publishing or distributing of statements), any political campaign on behalf of any candidate for public office.**

Mr. JOHNSON of Texas. Mr. President, **this amendment seeks to extend the provisions of section 501 of the House bill, denying tax-exempt status to not only those people who influence legislation but also to those who intervene in any political campaign on behalf of any candidate for any public office.**

I have discussed the matter with the chairman of the committee, the minority ranking member of the committee, and several other members of the committee, and I

Lyndon Baines Johnson

understand that the amendment is acceptable to them.

I hope the chairman will take it to conference, and that it will be included in the final bill which Congress passes.

Mr. MILLIKIN. Mr. President, I am willing to take the amendment to conference.

I understand from the minority leader that the distinguished Senator from Georgia [Mr. George] feels the same way about it.

The PRESIDING OFFICER. The question is on **agreeing to the amendment of the Senator from Texas [Mr. Johnson]. The amendment was agreed to.**

With no discussion, LBJ's amendment passed on a voice vote and 501(c)3 foundations were now limited from supporting candidates.

Why did LBJ introduce this Amendment? Did LBJ want a "separation of church and state"? Did he dislike churches? That would seen unlikely since his great-grandfather, George Washington Baines, was a Baptist preacher and president of Baylor University.

Franklin D. Roosevelt shaking hands with
Lyndon B. Johnson

TEXAS
VOTER FRAUD

"Voter fraud is no newcomer to the Lone Star State. Six decades ago, the votes 'found' in Jim Wells County's infamous Ballot Box 13 helped Lyndon Johnson squeak into the U.S. Senate."
- Texas Attorney General Greg Abbott, March 2006

A little background on LBJ's close elections gives insight into the motivation for his amendment.

LBJ was elected a Democrat Congressman from Texas in 1937 and was immediately noticed by Democrat President Franklin D. Roosevelt, who was elected the 32nd U.S. President in 1932.

During the Great Depression, FDR's "New Deal" big government programs were sufficiently to the left that many Socialist Party members supported FDR. Indeed, even Communist Party USA members supported FDR, especially during

Coke Stevenson
Democrat Governor of Texas
Candidate for U.S. Senate against LBJ

America's wartime alliance with the Soviet Union. In 1934, FDR said:

> A few timid people, who fear progress, will try to give you new and strange names for what we are doing. Sometimes they will call it **"Fascism,"** sometimes **"Communism,"** sometimes **"Socialism."** They are trying to make very complex and theoretical something that is really very practical... The real truth of the matter is that for a number of years in our country **the machinery of democracy had failed to function.**

Ronald Reagan remarked February 6, 1984:

> One commonly held view of the Roosevelt era was that **all societies were moving toward some modified form of communism.**

In 1941, **LBJ** ran for U.S. Senate. **FDR** made a speech on the eve of the election criticizing LBJ's opponent, Wilbert Lee O'Daniel, but LBJ lost by 1,311 votes. LBJ alleged voter fraud.

In 1948, LBJ ran for Senate again. On election night, September 2, 1948, in the Democrat Primary runoff against former Texas Governor Coke Stevenson, it appeared LBJ lost.

John B. Connally
LBJ's campaign manager 1948
Democrat Governor of Texas 1963-1969
On November 22, 1963, Connally was
shot in the same car in which
John F. Kennedy was assassinated.
Connally filed for bankruptcy in 1986.

Then, mysteriously, a box of uncounted ballots was "discovered" in the south Texas town of Alice in Jim Wells County, Precinct 13. Confusion reigned in Texas and by the end of the week, LBJ won by 87 votes. Both sides accused the other of voter fraud.

The FBI, Postal Department and other agencies investigated. Piecing together the details, the story emerged alleging that during the tabulation period, LBJ's campaign manager, John B. Connally, traveled to Alice, Texas.

With access granted by wealthy "political boss" of Duval County, George Parr, who later committed suicide, John Connally was present when the ballots were recounted and the returns amended.

When the dust settled, the new totals showed 202 additional voters, some of whom were deceased and buried in the local cemetery or were absent from the county on election day. These voters "lined up" in alphabetical order at the last minute, signed in the same blue ink in the same handwriting and cast their ballots for LBJ.

The Democrat Central Committee was deadlocked 28 to 28 on whether to certify the questionable election results, so Connally persuaded Frank W. Mayborn, publisher of the *Temple Daily Telegram*, to cut short a business trip in Nashville, Tennessee, and return to cast the deciding Committee vote to certify the election results.

Abe Fortas, FDR appointee, friend of LBJ,
U.S. Supreme Court Justice 1965-1969

Hugo Black, U.S. Supreme Court Justice
nominated by FDR in 1937

Coke Stevenson took LBJ to court and on September, 24, 1948, Judge T. Whitfield Davidson ordered LBJ's name removed from the general election ballot. LBJ turned to Washington attorney and former FDR appointee Abe Fortas.

Abe Fortas persuaded Supreme Court Justice Hugo Black, who was also appointed by FDR, to intervene. On September 28, 1948, Justice Black overturned the lower court ruling, letting the decision in the Johnson-Stevenson race rest with the Texas Democrat Central Committee.

In 1965, Abe Fortas was nominated by President Lyndon Johnson to be a Justice on the U.S. Supreme Court. During LBJ's term as President, many records of LBJ's contested race disappeared.

In 1966, Abe Fortas accepted money from a Wall Street financier investigated for securities violations. Abe Fortas resigned in 1969.

In March 2006, Texas Attorney General Greg Abbott posted a column on the Texas State Attorney General's website, stating:

> Voter fraud is no newcomer to the Lone Star State. Six decades ago, the votes 'found' in Jim Wells County's infamous Ballot Box 13 helped Lyndon Johnson squeak into the U.S. Senate [in] that 1948 primary.

Mao Zedong

Joseph Stalin

COMMUNISM

"Communism subjects the individual to arrest without lawful cause, punishment without trial, and forced labor as a chattel of the state."
- Harry S Truman, January 20, 1949, Inaugural Address

LBJ's 1948 election irregularities would probably have drifted into obscurity had it not been for a growing national anti-Communist movement, later referred to as McCarthyism or the Red Scare, which targeted his 1954 re-election.

One cannot appreciate the role "anti-Communists" played in LBJ's decision to introduce his IRS Amendment without understanding the prevailing national sentiment towards Communism.

As the Cold War began, an estimated 25 million Ukrainians died under Stalin's Communist purge in the U.S.S.R. and an estimated 80 million died under Mao Zedong's Communist cultural revolution in China.

Harry S Truman, 33rd U.S. President

Herbert Hoover, 31st U.S. President

In November 1956, Soviet Communists crushed Hungary, killing 2,500, wounding 13,000 and causing 200,000 to flee as refugees. Eventually, **over 45 countries fell to Communism**, including:

Afghanistan, Albania, Angola, Armenia, Azerbaijan, Belarus, Benin, Bosnia, Bulgaria, Cambodia, China, Congo, Cuba, Croatia, Czech Republic, East Germany, Eritrea, Estonia, Ethiopia, Georgia, Herzegovina, Hungary, Kazakhstan, Kyrgyzstan, Laos, Latvia, Lithuania, Macedonia, Moldova, Mongolia, Montenegro, Mozambique, North Korea, Poland, Romania, Russia, Serbia, Slovakia, Slovenia, Somalia, Tajikistan, Turkmenistan, Ukraine, Uzbekistan, Vietnam, and Yemen.

Harry S Truman stated January 20, 1949, in his Inaugural Address:

We believe that all men are created equal because they are created in the image of God. From this faith we will not be moved....

Communism is based on the belief that man is so weak and inadequate that he is unable to govern himself, and therefore requires the rule of strong masters.

Democracy is based on the conviction that man has the moral and intellectual capacity, as well as the inalienable right, to govern himself with reason and justice.

Communism subjects the individual to arrest without lawful cause, punishment without trial, and forced labor as a chattel of the state. It decrees what information he shall receive, what art he shall produce, what leaders he shall follow, and what thoughts he shall think.

Democracy maintains that government is established for the benefit of the individual, and is charged with the responsibility of protecting the rights of the individual and his freedom...

These differences between communism and democracy do not concern the United States alone. People everywhere are coming to realize that what is involved is material well-being, human dignity, and the right to believe in and worship God.

In 1950, the United Nations' New York headquarters was completed, thanks to a $8.5 million donation from John D. Rockefeller, Jr.:

On April 27, 1950, Herbert Hoover addressed the American Newspaper Publishers:

> What the world needs today is a...spiritual mobilization of the nations who believe in God against this **tide of Red agnosticism**.
>
> It needs a moral mobilization against **the hideous ideas of the police state and human slavery**...
>
> I suggest that the **United Nations should be reorganized without the Communist nations**...
>
> If that is impractical, then a definite **New United Front** should be organized of those peoples who disavow **Communism**, who stand for morals and religion, and who love freedom...It is a proposal for moral and spiritual cooperation of God-fearing free nations.
>
> And in rejecting an atheistic other world, I am confident that the Almighty God will be with us.

Herbert Hoover stated at a reception for his 80th birthday, August 10, 1954, West Branch, IA:

> **I have witnessed on the ground in 20 nations the workings of the philosophy of that anti-Christ, Karl Marx**...

Today the **Socialist virus and poison gas generated by Karl Marx and Friedrich Engels have spread into every nation on the earth.**

Their dogma is absolute materialism which defies truth and religious faith...

God has blessed us with another wonderful word, heritage. **The great documents of that heritage are not from Karl Marx. They are from the Bible, the Declaration of Independence and the Constitution...**Within them alone can the safeguards of freedom survive.

In 1945, Alexander Solzhenitsyn was arrested in Russia for writing a letter criticizing Communist leader Joseph Stalin and spent eleven years in labor camps. Solzhenitsyn began writing and eventually received the Nobel Prize for Literature. Solzhenitsyn wrote:

At the height of **Stalin's terror in 1937-38...more than 40,000 persons were shot per month**...Over there people are groaning and dying and in psychiatric hospitals, doctors are making their evening rounds, injecting people with drugs which destroy their brain cells.

You know the words from the Bible: "Build not on sand, but on rock"...**Lenin's teachings are that anyone is considered to be a fool who doesn't take what's lying in front of him.** If you can take it, take it. If you can attack, attack. But if there's a wall, then go back.

And the **Communist leaders respect only firmness and have contempt and laugh at persons who continually give in to them.**

America...they are trying to weaken you; they are trying to disarm your strong and magnificent country...I call upon you: ordinary working men of America...do not let yourselves become weak."

On January 25, 1952, the Religious Herald, Virginia, quoted Dwight Eisenhower in its article Presidential Candidates Stress Role of Religion:

What is our battle against **Communism** if it is not a fight between anti-God and a belief in the Almighty?...

Communists ... have to eliminate God from their system. When God comes, **Communism** has to go.

Solzhenitsyn spent 11 years in Communist labor camp

Dwight Eisenhower, 34th U.S. President

WILLIAM J. FEDERER, ENDANGERED SPEECHES-HOW THE

On June 5, 1952, Dwight Eisenhower spoke at Eisenhower Park in Abilene, Kansas *(TIME Magazine,* June 16, 1952):

> **China was lost to the free world** in one of the **greatest international disasters of our time** - a type of tragedy that must not be repeated.

On June 6, 1952, Dwight Eisenhower spoke in Abilene's Plaza Theater *(TIME,* June 16, 1952):

> Any kind of **Communistic, subversive or pinkish influence [must] be uprooted** from the responsible places in our government. Make no mistake about that.

Eisenhower told Congress, February 2, 1953:

> Our country has come through a painful period of trial and disillusionment since the victory of 1945...The calculated pressures of aggressive **Communism** have forced us...to live in a world of turmoil...
>
> No single country, even one so powerful as ours, can alone defend the liberty of all nations threatened by **Communist** aggression from without and **subversion within**...

I must make special mention of the war in **Korea.** This war is, for Americans, the most painful phase of **Communist** aggression throughout the world.

It is clearly a part of the same **calculated assault that the aggressor** is simultaneously pressing in **Indochina and in Malaya.**

Dwight Eisenhower sent a letter to the Senate, February 20, 1953:

The **Soviet Communist Party** who now control **Russia** ... subjected whole nations to the domination of a **totalitarian imperialism.**

In a February 25, 1953, Press Conference, Dwight Eisenhower stated:

Almost 100 percent of Americans would like to **stamp out all traces of Communism in our country...**

I went to Columbia University as its President and I insisted on one thing ... If we had a known **Communist** in our faculty and he could not be discharged ... I was automatically discharged.

I personally would not be a party to an organization where there was a known card-carrying

Communist in such a responsible position as teaching our young.

Eisenhower told reporters, March 5, 1953:

> Q. Mr. Reston: Do you regard the activities of the Tudeh party - the **Communist Party in Iran** - as an internal situation?
>
> THE PRESIDENT: In any country where a **Communist Party** is recognized...it is an internal situation.

At a News Conference, March 9, 1953, Eisenhower stated:

> Q. Mr. President, are you in favor of the Federal Government investigating **communism** in churches?
>
> THE PRESIDENT: I believe that if our churches - which certainly should be the greatest possible opponents to **communism** - need investigation, then we had better take a new look and go far beyond investigation in our country, in our combating of this what we consider a disease.
>
> Because the church, with its testimony of the existence of an Almighty God is the last thing that it seems to me would be preaching, teaching or tolerating **communism**.

Dwight Eisenhower
34th President
United States of America

So therefore I can see no possible good to be accomplished by questioning the loyalty of our churches in that regard.

Eisenhower told Congress, May 5, 1953:

In **Greece**, the onrush of **Communist** imperialism has been halted and forced to recede.

Out of the ruins left by that aggression, a proud, self-reliant nation has reestablished itself...

We are proposing to make substantial additional resources available to **assist the French** and the Associated States in their military efforts to defeat the **Communist Viet Minh aggression**.

At the College of William and Mary, May 15, 1953, Dwight Eisenhower stated:

It is necessary that we earnestly **seek out and uproot any traces of communism** at any place where it can affect our national life.

But the true way to **uproot communism in this country** is to understand what freedom means, and thus develop an impregnable wall, that no thought of communism can enter.

Cardinal Mindszenty was arrested by
Communists in Hungary, 1945

Dwight Eisenhower stated December 24, 1953, lighting the National Christmas Tree:

The world still stands divided in two antagonistic parts. **Prayer places freedom and communism in opposition one to the other.**

The **Communist** can find no reserve of strength in prayer because his **doctrine of materialism** and statism **denies the dignity of man** and consequently the existence of **God.**

But in America...religious faith is the foundation of free government, so is prayer an indispensable part of that faith...

The founders of this, our country, came first to these shores in search of freedom...**to live...beyond the yoke of tyranny.**

Dwight Eisenhower wrote to the United Catholic Organization for Freeing Cardinal Joseph Mindszenty, February 1, 1954:

The **Communist** assault upon religious liberty and leadership in **Hungary** has failed to turn the **Hungarian** people from their faith in God.

The plight of **Cardinal Mindszenty** and of other churchmen who have suffered at the hands of the **Communists** has not been forgotten...

The spirit of these men has defied confinement by the **totalitarian State.** It has become, indeed, a symbol of faith and freedom for our times.

Dwight Eisenhower stated November 9, 1954, to the National Conference on the Spiritual Foundation of American Democracy:

We are attacked by the **Communists** who in their own documents state that capitalism - Democracy - carries within itself the seeds of its own destruction...

Fundamentally **Democracy is nothing in the world but a spiritual conviction, a conviction that each of us is enormously valuable because of a certain standing before our own God.**

Now ... any organization such as that is, to my mind, a dedicated, patriotic group that can well take the Bible in one hand and the flag in the other, and march ahead.

At a Commemorative Concert, October 23, 1960, John F. Kennedy stated:

> Americans will never...recognize **Soviet domination of Hungary.**
>
> **Hungary's** claim to independence and liberty is not based on sentiment or politics. It is deeply rooted in history, in culture and in law. No matter what sort of puppet government they may maintain, we do not mean to see that claim abandoned.
>
> Americans intend to hasten...the day when the men and women of **Hungary** will stand again in freedom and justice.

On June 26, 1963, John F. Kennedy spoke at the wall dividing free West Berlin from Communist East Berlin:

> There are many people...who really don't understand...what is the great issue between the free world and the **Communist** world. Let them come to Berlin.
>
> There are some who say **Communism** is the wave of the future. Let them come to Berlin...
>
> There are...a few who say that it is true that **Communism** is an evil system, but it permits us to make economic

John F. Kennedy condemned the Soviet Communist invasion of Hungary in 1956

Rev. Richard Wurmbrand spent 14 years in Communist prisons in Romania.

progress...Let them come to Berlin.
Freedom has its difficulties and
is not perfect, but we have never had
to put a wall up to keep our people in.

In 1948, Lutheran minister Richard Wurmbrand
was arrested by Communists in Romania and was
tortured 14 years in prison. His wife, Sabina, was sent to
labor camp. Receiving amnesty, he testified in 1965 before
the U.S. Senate's Internal Security Subcommittee. In 1967,
the Wurmbrand's formed *Jesus To The Communist World*,
renamed *Voice of the Martyrs*. Richard Wurmbrand wrote:

Every freedom-loving man
has two fatherlands; his own and
America...Only America has the
power and spiritual resources to
stand as a barrier between militant
Communism and the people of the
world. It is the last "dike" holding
back the rampaging floodwaters of
militant Communism. If it crumples,
there is no other dike, no other dam;
no other line of defense to fall back
upon. **America is the last hope
of millions of enslaved peoples**...
**I have seen fellow-prisoners
in Communist prisons beaten,
tortured, with 50 pounds of
chains on their legs - praying for
America**...that the dike will not
crumple; that it will remain free.

In 1956, Communists invaded Hungary -
25,000 were imprisoned,
200,000 fled as refugees.

On December 11, 1963, LBJ told the Joint Chiefs of Staff and Department of Defense:

We must press on with all our energy against **the spread of Communist subversion into South Viet-Nam**...and **against the spread of Communist subversion in the Caribbean.** In these two areas we must be constantly alert to every opportunity...to strengthen the forces of freedom.

Richard Nixon addressed the Meaning of Communism to Americans, August 21, 1960:

The **Communist** philosophy is...inconsistent with the ideal of freedom because it denies that there can be any standard of moral truth by which the actions of any given social order may be judged... **Communist** philosophy makes any coherent theory of freedom impossible...The actual structure of the **Soviet regime** is such that **no true sense of freedom can ever develop under it.**

George H.W. Bush told Amish and Mennonite leaders in Lancaster, PA, March 22, 1989:

Barbara and I went to

Pol Pot, Communist Cambodian leader,
killed millions

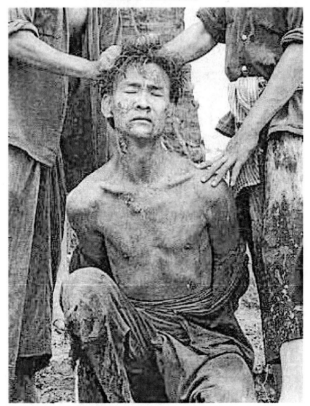

China as your emissary...**in 1974,** and we had wondered about the family in China - **Communist country, totalitarian...** We knew that there had been almost **entire banning on practicing and teaching Christianity...** This was right after the **Cultural Revolution.**

Gerald Ford requested Congress assist Vietnam and Cambodia, January 28, 1975:

Communists...violated the political provisions of the Paris Agreement. They have refused all **South Vietnamese** offers to set a specific date for free elections...

Recent events have made it clear that **North Vietnam** is again trying to impose a solution by force...

North Vietnamese forces captured an entire province, the population centers of which were clearly under the control of the **South Vietnamese Government...**

Communists have intensified hostilities by attacking on the outskirts of Phnom Penh and attempting to cut the land and water routes to the capital.

Ho Chi Minh,
Communist Vietnamese dictator

We must continue to **aid the Cambodian Government in the face of externally supported military attacks.**

Unless such assistance is provided, the Cambodian army will run out of ammunition...The Cambodian people are totally dependent on us for their only means of resistance to aggression.

Communist forces now attacking have a constant, massive outside source of supply from the North as has been demonstrated by their ability to sustain the current heavy offensive.

If additional military assistance is withheld or delayed, the Government forces will be forced, within weeks, to surrender.

Gerald Ford wrote to the Speaker of the House urging assistance, February 25, 1975:

I wish to convey...my deep concern over the...critical situation in Cambodia. An independent Cambodia cannot survive unless the Congress acts very soon...

Refugees forced to flee their homes by the **Communists'** repressive measures and scorched-

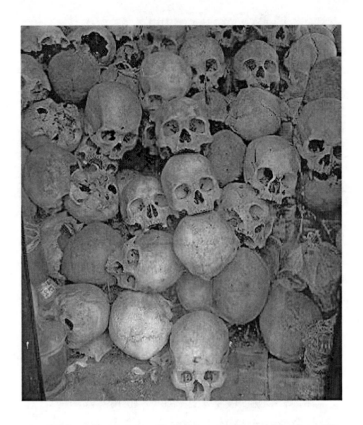

One-fifth of Cambodia's population - 1.7 million - were killed by Communist leader Pol Pot

earth policies have poured into Phnom Penh...

Severe food shortages are already beginning.

If the Congress does not provide for continued deliveries of...supplies, millions of innocent people will suffer - people who depend on us for their bare survival.

Gerald Ford spoke at a News Conference, March 6, 1975, on Cambodia and Vietnam:

On...assistance to **Cambodia and to Vietnam**...Food for those who hunger and medical supplies for the men and women and children who are suffering the ravages of war.

We seek to stop the bloodshed and end the horror and the tragedy that we see on television as rockets are fired wantonly into Phnom Penh.

I would like to be able to say that the killing would cease if we were to stop our aid, but that is not the case.

The record shows, in both Vietnam and Cambodia, that **Communist takeover** of an area **does not bring an end to violence,** but on the contrary, **subjects the innocent to new horrors.**

Over 5 million Vietnamese and Cambodians were
killed following France's withdrawal from Vietnam
in 1954 and Communists taking control

Jimmy Carter stated in his News Conference, March 24, 1977:

> There is an ideological struggle that has been in progress for decades between the **Communist** nations on the one hand and the **democratic nations** on the other.

Jimmy Carter stated to European Broadcast Journalists, May 2, 1977:

> We strongly favor the election of leaders who are committed to **freedom and democracy** and who are free from **Communist** philosophy, which quite often has been **dominated from the Soviet Union or other nations.**

Jimmy Carter stated to European Newspaper Journalists, April 25, 1977:

> The best way we can prevent the enhancement of **Communist** political strength in Europe is to show that democratically controlled governments can function effectively...
> To the extent that we fail as democracies...to live up to the ideals that exemplify our own commitments...we open the opportunity for **Communist** parties to be more successful.

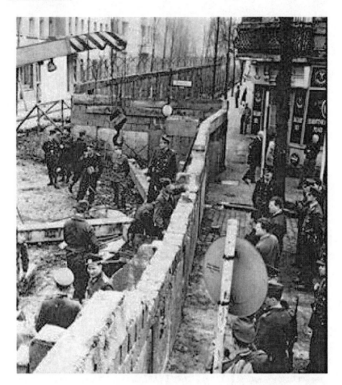

Communists building the Berlin Wall in 1961.

Communist Cuban dictator Fidel Castro

Ronald Reagan spoke to the British Parliament, June, 1982:

> The march of freedom and democracy which will leave **Marxism-Leninism** on the ashheap of history as it has left other **tyrannies which stifle the freedom and muzzle the self-expression of the people.**

Ronald Reagan stated at the Brandenburg Gate of the Berlin Wall in 1987:

> General Secretary Gorbachev, if you seek peace, if you seek prosperity for the **Soviet Union** and Eastern Europe, if you seek liberalization: Come here to this gate! Mr. Gorvachev, open this gate! Mr. Gorbachev, tear down this wall.

Ronald Reagan told the National Association of Evangelicals in Columbus, Ohio, March 6, 1984:

> We will deal with the **Communist** world as we must with a great power: by negotiating with it, from strength and in good faith...
> In our own hemisphere, the **Communist Sandinista regime in Nicaragua** has systematically violated human rights, including

Ronald Reagan at Berlin Wall's
Brandenburg Gate

the freedom to worship. Threats and harassment have forced virtually all **Nicaraguan Jews** to flee that country.

Catholic clerics have been attacked by government-instigated mobs. Protestant religious leaders have been arrested, beaten, and deported. Dozens of Protestant churches have been burned.

And today, **the Sandinistas are trying to spread Communist subversion throughout Central America. If they succeed, millions of Central Americans will suffer.**

And our own security and economy, especially in our own southern States, would be threatened by significantly increased numbers of refugees that might stream toward the United States.

During the Vietnam War, Admiral Jeremiah Denton had been a naval aviator and was shot down on July 18, 1965.

He was tortured in a Communist prison for eight years, which he detailed in his book, *When Hell Was In Session* (1998). After the War, he was elected a U.S. Senator from Alabama.

Admiral Jeremiah Denton's story is similar to that of naval aviator Captain John McCain, who was shot down during the Vietnam War, tortured in Communist prison for six years and later was elected a U.S. Senator from Arizona.

Explaining how Communism spread in Latin America, Admiral Jeremiah Denton wrote a draft for new chapter, titled "A Single Poker Hand," in which he stated:

> It was a terrible nightmare that President Carter had chosen to support the **Communist Sandinistas in Nicaragua, backed by the USSR...**
>
> I never dreamed of getting into politics, but when I saw **Ronald Reaga**n...I knew he was what the country desperately needed. **His early work against Communism in Hollywood really impressed me...**
>
> I was elected to the Senate and found myself again in a position to serve my country...
>
> Fidel Castro of Cuba was personally in charge of swapping arms to the Colombians in exchange for drugs that he smuggled into the U.S., while the

Columbians transferred plenty of arms to the Sandinistas for their mischief in El Slavador.

In the mid 1980's, during a tense moment in international relations, Senator Jeremiah Denton, with approval from President Reagan, went to Nicaragua and confronted the Nicaraguan Communist government, causing its leader, Daniel Ortega, to lose face.

This was a turning point in stemming the aggressive spread of Communism in Latin America.

Only recently has Communism been experiencing a resurgence in Latin America, due to the efforts of Hugo Chavez of Venezuela, financed through his country's oil and his connections with Cuba, Russia, Iran and China.

Admiral Jeremiah Denton

Whitaker Chambers, a Communist spy who
defected to the United States, testified before the
House Un-American Activities Committee in 1948.

WHITTAKER CHAMBERS

"At a critical moment in our Nation's history, Whittaker Chambers stood alone against the brooding terrors of our age...

He became the focus of a momentous controversy in American history that symbolized our century's epic struggle between freedom and totalitarianism."

- Ronald Reagan, March 26, 1984, Ceremony Presenting Medal of Freedom to Whittaker Chambers

Whittaker Chambers began attending New York's Columbia University in 1921.

In 1924, he read Lenin's *Soviets at Work* (1919) and in 1925 joined the Communist Party USA. He wrote and edited the Communist publications *The Daily Worker* newspaper and *The New Masses* magazine.

He translated from German into English the 1923 book *Bambi, ein Leben im Walde* (*Bambi, A Life in the Woods*), which Walt Disney Productions turned into an animated film in 1942, though much less dark and brutal than the book.

By 1932, Whittaker Chambers had joined the Communist underground and lived a life of espionage, working with spies in Franklin D. Roosevelt's New Deal administration, smuggling documents to Communists.

When several fellows spies were found murdered after Stalin had begun his Great Purge, which killed millions in the U.S.S.R., Chambers went into hiding in 1937.

In 1939, Chambers joined the staff of *TIME Magazine* and eventually rose to be a senior editor. After another Soviet spy who defected, Walter Krivitsky, was found murdered in 1941, Whittaker Chambers decided to meet with the FBI in 1942.

The FBI did not take him seriously until another spy, Elizabeth Bentley defected in 1945 and corroborated Chambers' story.

In 1948, Whittaker Chambers testified before the House Un-American Activities Committee, naming 18 current and former government employees as Communist spies or sympathizers, including Alger Hiss.

After his death, Whittaker Chambers was awarded the Medal of Freedom by Ronald Reagan. At the Presentation Ceremony, March 26, 1984, Ronald Reagan remarked

The Medal of Freedom is designed not to honor individuals for single acts of bravery, but instead, to acknowledge lifetime accomplishments that have changed the face and the soul of our country...
At a critical moment in our Nation's history, Whittaker Chambers stood alone against the brooding terrors of our age.
Consummate intellectual, writer of moving majestic prose, and witness to the truth, **he became the focus of a momentous controversy in American history that symbolized our century's epic struggle between freedom and totalitarianism,** a controversy in which the solitary figure of **Whittaker Chambers** personified the mystery of human redemption in the face of evil and suffering.
As long as humanity speaks of virtue and **dreams of freedom,** the life and writings of **Whittaker Chambers** will ennoble and inspire.

Ronald Reagan remarked at the Annual Convention of the National Association of Evangelicals in Columbus, Ohio, March 6, 1984:

> **Whittaker Chambers understood the struggle between totalitarianism and the West.**
>
> **He, himself, had turned to communism out of a sense of idealism** in which he thought that might be the answer.
>
> And then he wrote, all the great visions of the free world "have always been different versions of the same vision: the vision of God and man's relationship to God. **The Communist vision is the vision of man without God.**"...
>
> **When men try to live in a world without God,** it's only too easy for them to **forget the rights that God bestows**—too easy to suppress freedom of speech, to build walls to keep their countrymen in, to jail dissidents, and to put great thinkers in mental wards.

Ronald Reagan remarked at Eureka College in Eureka, Illinois, February 6, 1984:

An editor of *TIME* magazine, Whittaker Chambers, in public testimony in 1948 named former high U.S. Government officials as spies.

He was not believed at first, but the...overwhelming evidence led a jury to convict one of those former officials of perjury.

In Chambers' autobiography, "Witness," he added a sequel.

Chambers marked the beginning of his personal journey away from communism on the day that he was suddenly struck by the sight of his infant daughter's ear as she sat there having breakfast...

He said, he realized that such intricacy, such precision could be no accident, no freak of nature...

He didn't know it at the time, in that moment, God—the finger of God had touched his forehead.

And that is why Chambers would write that faith, not economics, is the central problem of our age...

The western world does not know it, but it already possesses **the answer to this problem,** he said, but only **provided that its faith in God... is as great as communism's belief in material power.**

Ronald Reagan remarked at a Conservative Political Action Conference Dinner, Mayflower Hotel, Washington, DC, February 26, 1982:

Whittaker Chambers... sought idealism in communism and found only disillusionment...
He wrote, "For in this century, within the next decades, will be decided for generations **whether all mankind is to become Communist,** whether the whole world is to become free, or whether in the struggle civilization as we know it is to be completely destroyed or completely changed.
It is our fate to live upon that turning point in history.

On March 20, 1981, at the Conservative Political Action Conference Dinner, Mayflower Hotel, Washington, DC, Ronald Reagan stated:

Evil is powerless if the good are unafraid.

That's why the **Marxist vision of man without God** must eventually be seen as an empty and a false faith—the second oldest in the world—first proclaimed in the Garden of Eden with whispered words..."Ye shall be as gods."

The crisis of the Western world, Whittaker Chambers reminded us, exists to the degree in which it is indifferent to God.

Ronald Reagan remarked to Administration Officials on Domestic Policy, December 13, 1988:

Whittaker Chambers once wrote that, in his words, **"Human societies, like human beings, live by faith and die when faith dies."**

Ronald Reagan remarked at the Annual Convention of the National Association of Evangelicals in Orlando, Florida, March 8, 1983:

Whittaker Chambers...wrote that the crisis of the Western World exists to the degree...it collaborates in communism's attempt to make man stand alone without God...

I believe that **communism is another sad, bizarre chapter in human history.**

Alger Hiss, who helped write the U.N. Charter,
was accused of being a Communist spy
and convicted of perjury.

ALGER HISS

"Whittaker Chambers...
own religious conversion made
him a witness to one of the
terrible traumas of our time,
the Hiss-Chambers case."
- Ronald Reagan, March 8,
1983, National Association of
Evangelicals Convention, Orlando, FL

Alger Hiss received a law degree from
Harvard, where he was the protege' of ACLU
attorney Felix Frankfurter, who was
nominated to the Supreme Court by Franklin
D. Roosevelt.

In 1936, Alger Hiss went to work for
the U.S. State Department during Franklin
D. Roosevelt's New Deal Administration.

Alger Hiss had been at the secret Yalta
Conference, February 4 to February 11, 1945,
where Franklin Roosevelt, Winston Churchill
and Joseph Stalin divided up post-war
Europe.

The Yalta Conference determined which countries of Europe would be free and which would be Communist.

In 1945, Alger Hiss was secretary general of the United Nations Conference on International Organization, where he helped write the United Nations' Charter.

Alger Hiss then served as United Nations Director of the Office of Special Political Affairs.

Regarding the United Nations, President Dwight Eisenhower told the Annual Convention of the National Junior Chamber of Commerce, Minneapolis, Minnesota, June 10, 1963:

> From its foundation the **United Nations** has seemed to be **two distinct things to the two worlds divided by the iron curtain...**
>
> **To the free world** it has seemed that it should be **a constructive forum** for free distribution of the world's problems, **an effective agency for helping to solve those problems peacefully...**

To the Communist world it has been a **convenient sounding board for their propaganda, a weapon to be exploited in spreading disunity and confusion.**

In 1946, Alger Hiss became President of the globalist Carnegie Endowment for International Peace, a 501(c)3 Foundation.

On August 3, 1948, Whittaker Chambers, who had defected from being a Communist spy, accused Alger Hiss of also being a Communist spy, with the role of promoting Communist policies in FDR's New Deal Government.

Based on Chamber's accusation, and testimony of other defected Communist spies, Elizabeth Bentley, Igor Gouzenko and Hede Massing, Alger Hiss was tried and convicted of perjury in a very public trial on January 25, 1950.

Testimony in 1952 from defected Communist spy, Nathaniel Weyl, a 1985 book by KGB Oleg Gordievsky, and Hungarian Communist records discovered in 1992 of spy Noel Field, corroborated Whittaker Chambers' accounts.

LBJ

ANTI-COMMUNISM & LBJ'S RE-ELECTION

"*A* *vote for Johnson - many Texans feel - will be a vote for more centralization of power and socialism...for more covering up of Communist infiltration.*"
- Willis Ballinger, "The Texas Story," circulated by 501(c)3 Committee for Constitutional Government, 1954

After the trial of Alger Hiss, an intense anti-Communist sentiment swept America.

A young Congressman from California, Richard Nixon, became a leader in the anti-Communist movement. Two weeks after the Alger Hiss verdict, Wisconsin Senator Joseph McCarthy gave a famous anti-Communist speech in Wheeling, West Virginia, which defined the era.

Frank Gannett,
New York Publisher
Founded the Committee
for Constitutional Government

In response to the rapid expansion of Communism worldwide, educational 501(c)3 foundations began to be formed in the United States to educate the public to this growing threat.

New York publisher Frank E. Gannett founded the Committee for Constitutional Government and Texas oil millionaire H.L. Hunt founded the FACTS FORUM.

LBJ was intent on continuing FDR's big government "New Deal" agenda which he later called "The Great Society."

LBJ stated in Mexico City, April 15, 1966:

My administration...will not be deterred by those who say that to risk **change** is to risk **communism.**

The Committee for Constitutional Government and the FACTS FORUM made numerous reports on LBJ, accusing him of holding communist-leaning political views and accusing him of election irregularities in past close elections.

LBJ, now the youngest Democrat Senate Minority Leader in history, was becoming concerned that these negative reports would result in another close election.

H.L. Hunt, Texas oil millionaire
Founded the FACTS FORUM

An example of these reports was an article titled "The Texas Story" written by Willis Ballinger (*Spotlight for the Nation*, No. D-269),: and circulated in 1954 by the 501(c)3 Committee for Constitutional Government.

Cited in Mark Eldon Young's 1993 University of Texas Masters Thesis, *Lyndon B. Johnson's Forgotten Campaign: Re-election to the Senate in 1954,* Willis Ballinger wrote:

> **A vote for Johnson** - many Texans feel - will be **a vote for** more centralization of power and **socialism in Washington**; for more of the **internationalism** which is designed to **abolish the U.S.A.**; and for more covering up of **Communist infiltration.**

As his 1954 re-election approached, LBJ grew more nervous and pursued ways to silence the FACTS FORUM and Committee for Constitutional Government.

LBJ wrote to the Senate Democratic Policy Committee counsel, Gerald Seigel, asking if the Committee for Constitutional Government had violated the Texas Election Code.

Gerald Seigel replied to LBJ in a memo, June 15, 1954 (Deirdre Halloran, *Free Exercise v. The Code: Restrictions on Church Political Activity,* March, 1996)

LBJ and JFK

The **Committee for Constitutional Government** has openly solicited corporate contributions to its organization for its **so-called educational purposes...**

In distributing this material in Texas it has clearly **engaged** in an indirect, if not direct, effort to influence a senatorial election... **attempting to defeat your candidacy.**

H.L Hunt, a friend of anti-Communist Senator Joseph McCarthy of Wisconsin, spent over four million dollars building the FACTS FORUM, an educational 501(c)3 foundation.

The FACTS FORUM had a nationwide mailing list of 60,000 monthly newsletter subscribers and 125,000 "participants."

The FACTS FORUM aired a half-hour weekly program, "Answers for Americans," on 22 TV stations and 360 radio stations; and a weekly radio program, "State of the Nation," on 315 stations, a "both sides" program on 222 stations, and a half-hour TV show broadcast from Washington, D.C., on 58 TV stations.

Wayne Hays
Democrat Congressman from Ohio

The FACTS FORUM distributed public-opinion polls to 1,800 U.S. newspapers, 500 radio and TV stations and to every member of Congress.

In January 1954, a Providence, Rhode Island, newspaper, the *Journal-Bulletin*, assigned a young reporter, Ben H. Bagdikian, to do an investigative story on the FACTS FORUM.

Bagdikian's story claimed the FACTS FORUM was partisan. Soon similar articles appeared in *TIME* (Jan. 11, 1954), *U.S. News and World Report* (Jan. 28, 1954), *The Reporter* (Feb. 16, 1954) and *New Republic* (Feb. 22, 1954).

Democrat Rep. Wayne Hays of Ohio, a friend of LBJ who later resigned due to sex scandals, **asked the IRS to investigate the FACTS FORUM.**

Hays wanted the IRS to see if the FACTS FORUM's educational activities violated the 1934 IRS Code by substantially "influencing legislation." The IRS found no wrong doing.

A *New York Times* article June 4, 1954, stated:

The Internal Revenue Service, after a full investigation, had continued the tax-exemption of the FACTS FORUM Foundation.

LBJ

The Government was more concerned with uncovering Communists, as the House Select Committee to Investigate Tax-Exempt Foundations, formed in 1952 and chaired by Rep. Eugene E. Cox (R-GA), tried to determine:

...whether foundations have been infiltrated by Communists, as well as whether tax-exempt groups are using their money for stated purposes and are not endangering our existing capitalistic structure.

Though the Special Committee did not find direct subversion, it noted that foundations were vulnerable to such influence.

It also found some foundations, such as the Rockefeller Foundation, Carnegie Foundation and Ford Foundation, were becoming so powerful they could "materially influence public opinion."

The Committee's December 1954 report claimed these foundations were supporting left-leaning, socialist and collectivist ideologies.

Whereas the focus of the Special Committee was mostly on left-leaning foundations, Congressman Wayne Hays of Ohio, the leading Democrat on the Committee, used his powerful position to investigate the FACTS FORUM.

LBJ and Jacqueline Kennedy

When the Special Committee ended its investigative work on **July 2, 1954,** without finding fault with the 501(c)3 FACTS FORUM or the Committee for Constitutional Government, **LBJ pursued another avenue.**

That same day, July 2, 1954, LBJ proposed to silence those foundations by introducing in the Senate his amendment to remove the tax-exempt status of 501(c)3 foundations which intervened in political campaigns.

LBJ's amendment was adopted without hearings because both sides of the political fence wanted to curtail the influence of powerful 501(c)3 educational foundations.

LBJ wanted to limit right-leaning tax-exempt foundations like the FACTS FORUM and Committee for Constitutional Government, and the other side of the political aisle wanted to limit left-leaning tax-exempt foundations like the Rockefeller Foundation, Carnegie Foundation and Ford Foundation.

Congressman B. Carroll Reece, Chairman of the House Special Committee to Investigate Tax-Exempt Foundations, reported in American Mercury 56-64, July 1957, that through left-leaning tax-exempt foundations, the U.S. taxpayer was actually underwriting the spread of Communism.

Joseph McCarthy
U.S. Senator from Wisconsin 1947-1957
Chairman of the Senate Committee on
Government 1953-1957, where he appointed
27-year-old Robert Kennedy as assistant counsel

On February 28, 1957, the Senate Internal Security subcommittee of the Committee on the Judiciary recommended Congress withdraw tax-exempt status from any foundation:

> ...contributing funds to a Communist or Communist-front organization, or for Communist purposes.

After LBJ won re-election in 1954, and the Democrat Party gained control of the U.S. Senate, LBJ was chosen to be the youngest ever Democrat Senate Majority Leader.

LBJ immediately led the fight to censure Senator Joseph McCarthy, who had became unpopular with many for his zealous efforts to uncover Communist subversion.

At a News Conference at the LBJ Ranch, July 18, 1964, LBJ said:

> I have stated it on the floor of the Senate. I criticized Senator McCarthy for the practices he employed. I voted to censure him.

LBJ was successful in censuring McCarthy on December 2, 1954, thus ending McCarthy's career.

Vasili Mitrokhin, senior archivist for
the Soviet Union's foreign intelligence

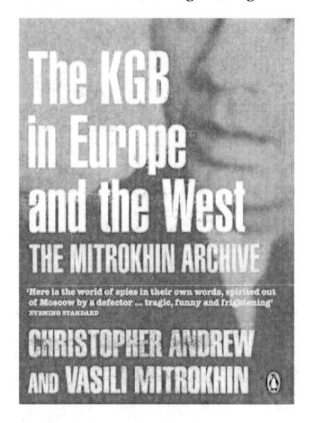

LBJ's efforts had the effect of ending the anti-Communist movement in the United States.

Senator Joseph McCarthy died less than three year later, on May 2, 1957.

Though Senator McCarthy has been "Blacklisted by History," as is the title of M. Stanton Evans' book, documents later released by the U.S.S.R. following the Cold War provided evidence that in numerous instances, Senator McCarthy suspicions of Communist infiltration appeared justified.

One such source was Vasili Mitrokhin, senior archivist for the Soviet Union's foreign intelligence and the First Chief Directorate of the KGB.

After the dismantling of the Berlin Wall in 1989 and the disestablishment of the Soviet Union in 1991, Vasili Mitrokhin left Russia for Estonia, then traveled to England in 1992.

Vasili Mitrokhin brought with him over 25,000 pages of Soviet intelligence documents, out of which he wrote the book *The Mitrokhin Archive: The KGB in Europe and the West* (1999), with co-author Christopher Andrew.

LBJ

ONE 501(C)3 SILENCES ANOTHER

*"**M**ost of the ACLU's litigation and communication efforts described in this Website are done by the ACLU Foundation...*

A donor may make a tax-deductible gift only to the ACLU Foundation."

\- www.ACLU.org

For years, churches had no realization that LBJ's amendment affected them.

Even LBJ's chief aide in 1954, George Reedy, wrote in personal correspondence with Deirdre Halloran (*Free Exercise v. The Code: Restrictions on Church Political Activity,* 1996), that he was "confident that Johnson would never have sought restrictions on religious organizations."

Rev. W.A. Criswell, pastor
First Baptist Church, Dallas

John F. Kennedy at the Greater Houston
Ministerial Association, September 12, 1960

Bruce R. Hopkins, in his book, *The Law of Tax-Exempt Organizations-6th Edition* (NY: John Wiley & Sons, 1992), claimed that LBJ's amendment was politically motivated.

In a personal telephone conversation, March 18, 1996, Bruce R. Hopkins reiterated his claim, saying it was based on a conversation with a former Congressional staff person who had actually worked with Lyndon Johnson on the language used in amendment.

That LBJ's Amendment was political and not anti-religious was repeated by Michael C. Hone, in *Aristotle and Lyndon Baines Johnson: Thirteen Ways of Looking at Blackbirds and Nonprofit Corporations* (The American Bar Association's Revised Model Nonprofit Corporation Act; *Case Western Reserve Law Review* 39:751-774, 1989.)

Churches continued to operate with their understanding that Congress could not prohibit their free exercise of religion or limit their freedom of speech, press and assembly.

As recent as July 3, 1960, Rev. W.A. Criswell preached a radio-broadcast sermon from the First Baptist Church in Dallas, Texas, stating he was against Catholic John F. Kennedy being President. H.L. Hunt financed sending thousands of copies of Rev. Criswell's sermon transcripts across the nation.

This was viewed as simply exercising freedoms pastors had always exercised from the founding of the nation, especially since the First Amendment came into being largely in response to Baptist preachers in Virginia, such as John Leland, convincing James Madison to introduce it to insure Baptists would not be persecuted under America's new government as they had been under King George III's Anglican government.

It was understood that the First Amendment limited the Federal "Congress," not churches.

John F. Kennedy rescued his Presidential campaign, September 12, 1960, by explaining to the Greater Houston Ministerial Association his version of separation of church and state:

> We have far more critical issues in the 1960 campaign - **the spread of Communist influence, until it festers only 90 miles from the coast of Florida**...But because I am Catholic, and no Catholic has ever been elected President...it is...necessary for me to state...what...I believe...
>
> I believe in an America where the separation of church and state is absolute; **where no Catholic prelate would tell the President... how to act...**

Where **no public official** either requests or **accepts instruction** on public policy **from the Pope...**

I would not look with favor upon a President working to subvert the First Amendment's guarantee of religious liberty...

But if the time should come...when my office would require me to either violate my conscience or violate the national interest, then I would resign the office.

In time, the IRS Tax Code grew more complex and pastors grew more complacent. Even legal scholar Judge Learned Hand had expressed dismay over the IRS Tax Code's growing complexity ("Thomas Walter Swan," 57 *Yale Law Journal*, No. 2, 167, 169, Dec.1947):

In my own case the words of such an act as the Income Tax... merely dance before my eyes in a meaningless procession: cross-reference to cross-reference, exception upon exception - couched in abstract terms that offer no handle to seize hold of, leave in my mind only a confused sense of some vitally important, but successfully concealed, purport, which it is my duty to extract, but which is within my

Judge Learned Hand

power, if at all, only after the most inordinate expenditure of time.

I know that these monsters are the result of fabulous industry and ingenuity, plugging up this hole and casting out that net, against all possible evasion; yet at times I cannot help recalling a saying of William James about certain passages of Hegel: that they were no doubt written with a passion of rationality; but that one cannot help wondering whether to the reader they have any significance save that the words are strung together with syntactical correctness.

In 1959, the Treasury Department began issuing complicated new regulations explaining the changes in the IRS Code, now with LBJ's 1954 Amendment.

The **ACLU 501(c)3 tax-exempt Foundation,** using these new regulations, began a program of **legal intimidation** of 501(c)3 tax-exempt churches and ministries.

Since churches did not want to lose their 501(c)3 tax-exempt status, pastors began refraining from speaking on public issues, effectively relinquishing their role as the conscience of society.

Roger Baldwin
Founder of the ACLU,
officed in the U.N. building and
awarded the Medal of Freedom
by Jimmy Carter, 1981

ACLU

"*I* wanted what the Communists wanted."
- Roger Baldwin, Founder of the ACLU 501(c)3 Foundation, in *Liberty Under the Soviets* 1927

The American Civil Liberties Union, or ACLU, is a 501(c)3 tax-exempt Foundation founded by Roger Baldwin, who gained notoriety by directing the Scopes Monkey Trial to get evolution taught in schools, eventually leading a ban on the teaching of creation.

Roger Baldwin was friends with Earl Browder, who served as the general secretary of the Communist Party USA from 1930 to its dissolution in 1944. The Communist Party USA was reconstituted in 1945.

Roger Baldwin twice visited the Soviet Union, embraced Vietnamese Communist dictator Ho Chi Minh, and wrote a book, *Liberty Under the Soviets* (1927), in which he stated:

Roger Baldwin, ACLU Founder

Ho Chi Minh
Vietnamese Communist dictator
visited by Roger Baldwin

I joined. I don't regret being a part of the **Communist** tactic, which increased the effectiveness of a good cause.

I knew what I was doing. I was not an innocent liberal. **I wanted what the Communists wanted.**

Baldwin's friend Emma Goldman, known as "Red Emma," was deported to the Soviet Union in 1919 for her Communist activities.

The on-line exhibit of Emma Goldman's papers claim her career:

...served as inspiration for Roger Baldwin, a future founder of the American Civil Liberties Union.

In 1935, Roger Baldwin wrote in the Harvard reunion book on the 30th reunion of his class of 1905:

I am for socialism, disarmament, and ultimately, for abolishing the state itself as an instrument of violence and compulsion.

I seek social ownership of property, the abolition of the properties class, and sole control of those who produce wealth. **Communism is the goal.**

A co-founder of the ACLU 501(c)3 tax-exempt Foundation with Roger Baldwin was William Z. Foster, National Chairman of the Communist Party USA.

In 1932, William Z. Foster wrote in *Toward Soviet America*:

> The establishment of an American Soviet government will involve the confiscation of large landed estates in town and country, and also, the whole body of forests, mineral deposits, lakes, rivers and so on.

Another co-founder of the ACLU 501(c)3 tax-exempt Foundation was Norman Thomas, who was the six-time Presidential candidate for the Socialist Party, 1928-1948. Norman Thomas stated:

> **The American people will never knowingly adopt socialism, but under the name of liberalism, they will adopt every fragment of the socialist program** until one day America will be a socialist nation without ever knowing how it happened.

Earl Browder, general secretary of the Communist Party USA, claimed the ACLU 501(c)3 tax-exempt Foundation was "a transmission belt" to help achieve the goals of Communism for America.

A list of 45 Communist goals, which can be compared with the ACLU agenda further in this chapter, was read into the Congressional Record, January 10, 1963, by Congressman Albert S. Herlong, Jr., of Florida (Vol 109, 88th Congress, 1st Session, Appendix, pp. A34-A35).

The list of Communist goals included:

Eliminate prayer or any phase of religious expression in the schools on the ground that it violates the principle of "separation of church and state."...
Eliminate laws governing obscenity by calling them "censorship" and a violation of free speech and free press...
Use technical decisions of the courts to weaken basic American institutions by claiming their activities violate civil rights...Discredit American culture...
Discredit the family as an institution. Encourage promiscuity and divorce...

Present homosexuality, degeneracy and promiscuity as "normal, natural, healthy."...

Emphasize the need to raise children away from the negative influence of parents...

Infiltrate churches and replace revealed religion with "social" religion...

Discredit the Bible and emphasize the need for intellectual maturity which does not need a "religious crutch.."..

Discredit the Constitution by calling it inadequate, old-fashioned, out of step with modern needs, a hindrance to cooperation between nations on a worldwide basis.

Discredit Founding Fathers. Present them as selfish aristocrats who had no concern for the "common man."...

Control schools. Use them as transmission belts for socialism and current Communist propaganda. Soften curriculum.

Get control of teachers' associations. Put party line in textbooks... Control student newspapers...

Infiltrate the press... Control book-review assignments, editorial writing, policymaking positions...

Control key positions in radio, TV and motion pictures...

Break down cultural standards of morality by promoting pornography and obscenity in books, magazines, motion pictures, radio and TV...

Belittle all forms of American culture and discourage the teaching of American history on the ground that it was only a minor part of the "big picture."...

Support socialist movement to give centralized control over any part of the culture - education, social agencies, welfare programs, mental health clinics, etc. ...

Transfer some of the power of arrest from the police to social agencies...

Dominate the psychiatric profession and use mental health laws as a means of gaining coercive control over those who oppose Communist goals.

Infiltrate and control of more unions. Infiltrate and gain control of big business....

Promote the U.N...

In 1950, members of the Communist Party USA formed America's **first** homosexual rights orgniazation - rights which the ACLU defends.

Free trade, loans and aid to all nations regardless of Communist affiliation...

Internationalize the Panama Canal ... Give the World Court jurisdiction...

Do away with loyalty oaths.... Capture one or both of the political parties...

Eliminate the House Committee on Un-American Activities... Resist any attempt to outlaw the Communist Party.

In 1948, the California Senate Fact Finding Committee on Un-American Activities stated in its report, page 107:

The ACLU may be definitely classified as a Communist front or transmission belt organization...
At least 90 percent of its efforts are on behalf of Communists who come in conflict with the law.

In 1950, members of the Communist Party USA formed **the Mattachine Society, the nation's first homosexual rights organizations**. which lobbied to repeal sodomy laws.

On January 17, 1931, the Special House Committee to Investigate Communist Activities issued a report stating:

> **The American Civil Liberties Union is closely affiliated with the communist movement in the United States, and fully 90% of its efforts are on behalf of Communists who have come into conflict with the law.**
>
> It claims to stand for free speech, free press, and free assembly; but it is quite apparent that **the main function of the ACLU is to attempt to protect the Communists** in their advocacy of force and violence to overthrow the Government, replacing the American flag with a red flag and **erecting a Soviet Government** in place of the **republican form of government** guaranteed **to each State** by the **Federal Constitution...**
>
> **Roger N. Baldwin,** its guiding spirit, **makes no attempt to hide his friendship for the Communists** and their principles.

The 87th Congress Congressional Record, September 20, 1961, recorded remarks of Hon. John H. Rousselot of California, which included the House Committee To Investigate Communist Activities in the United States report 2290, entitled "Investigation of Communist Propaganda":

> **The main function of the ACLU is to protect the Communists** in their advocacy of force and violence to overthrow the U.S. Government.

In 1939, Roger Baldwin felt Russia's Communist leader Joseph Stalin had compromised Communism's high ideals by signing a pact with the fascist leader of Nazi Germany, Adolph Hitler.

In the 1940's, in an effort to mitigate growing negative public opinion, Roger Baldwin attempted to reinvent his organization's image by distancing himself from visible Communists, though the agenda of the ACLU 501(c)3 tax-exempt Foundation remained unchanged.

By examining the total volume of ACLU 501(c)3 tax-exempt Foundation cases, two categories emerge: those the ACLU is against and those the ACLU defends.

The ACLU defended Nazi demostrators in
Skokie, Illinois, 1978.

The Blues Brothers (1980)

By connecting the dots, with a few exceptions, a pattern emerges, namely that the ACLU is promoting a consistent partisan agenda.

For example, the ACLU 501(c)3 tax-exempt Foundation sued to remove: school prayer, Christmas carols, Ten Commandment displays, Boy Scouts, "under God" in the Pledge of Allegiance, nativity scenes, abstinence education, religious symbols from city seals and veterans memorials, prayer at Naval Academy, and is against private gun ownership and against private rights of conscience for pro-life doctors.

Yet the ACLU 501(c)3 tax-exempt Foundation defended: Communists, Nazis, KKK members, the North American Man Boy Love Association, pornographers, gay, lesbian, bisexual, transgender, abortion, Islamic terrorists, no identification to vote, gay marriage and burning the American Flag.

A notable case took place in 1978 when the ACLU 501(c)3 tax-exempt Foundation defended a group of Nazis who wanted to demonstrate in the largely Jewish community of Skokie, Illinois.

This incident was humorously alluded to in the movie The Blues Brothers (1980) with Dan Aykroyd and John Belushi driving their Bluesmobile over a Chicago bridge causing Nazi demonstrators to jump into the river.

In spite of its website saying: "We are nonprofit and nonpartisan," the ACLU 501(c)3 tax-exempt Foundation appears consistent in its support of a particular partisan political agenda.

The ACLU's partisan agenda is nearly identical to that of the Communist Party USA and one of America's two major political parties, as well as the stated political agenda of its contributors, such as the 501(c)3 Gill Foundation, whose website states:

> The Gill Foundation... invested more than $120 million **to support ... nonprofit organizations...that share its commitment** to equal rights for lesbian, gay, bisexual and transgender Americans.

Just as H.L. Hunt's 501(c)3 tax-exempt foundation, FACTS FORUM, with its national influence and multi--million dollar budget, was investigated for being "partisan," the ACLU 501(c)3 tax-exempt Foundation, with its national influence and multi-million dollar budget, may warrant an investigation for being "partisan."

Additionally, since ACLU lawsuits often result in judges effectively creating law, legislating from the bench, it is legitimate to ask if the ACLU 501(c)3 tax-exempt Foundation is violating the 1934 Revenue Act by "substantially influencing legislation."

CONTINUING COMMUNIST CONNECTIONS

"From now on I knew I would be described as a Communist, but frankly I had reached the stage where I didn't give a damn."
- Frank Marshall Davis

Since the ACLU 501(c)3 tax-exempt Foundation and the Communist Party USA share an intertwined past, it is interesting to trace some continuing communist connections of recent history.

In 1956, the Senate Internal Security Subcommittee reported:

Founded in September 1919, the Communist Party of the United States of America is an organization unique in American history.

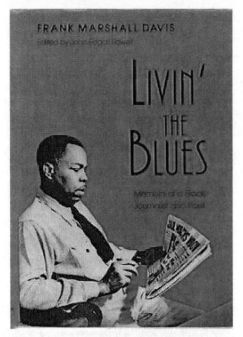

Frank Marshall Davis

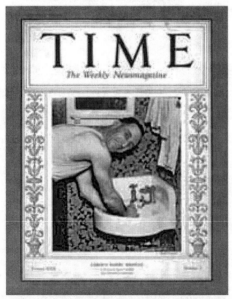

Harry Bridges, Communist editor of
the *Honolulu Record*

It is not a true political party and differs fundamentally from all political parties in this country.

It is in fact a Russian-inspired, Moscow-dominated military conspiracy against our Government, our ideals, and our freedoms.

FRANK MARSHALL DAVIS

Accuracy in Media's newsletter AIM Report, written by editor Cliff Kincaid (September 2008) described some Communist Party USA members.

In 1956, known Communist Party USA member Frank Marshall Davis appeared before the Senate Internal Security Subcommittee, pleading the Fifth Amendment, which states: "No person...shall be compelled in any criminal case to be a witness against himself."

Frank Marshall Davis studied journalism at Kansas State University in 1924-27, then moved to Chicago as a writer. He moved to Atlanta, then back to Chicago where, in 1943, he joined the Communist Party USA.

In her article "Frank Marshall Davis: A Forgotten Voice in the Chicago Black Renaissance," written by ex-University of Hawaii professor Kathryn Takara (2002), Davis is quoted as saying:

From now on I knew I would be described as a Communist, but frankly I had reached the stage where I didn't give a damn.

After the 1948 testimony of Whittaker Chambers, the anti-Communist movement in the United States rapidly grew, resulting in many Communists moving to Hawaii, a less regulated U.S. Territory which did not become the 50th State until 1959.

In 1948, Frank Marshall Davis moved to Hawaii.

In *Political Affairs*, the journal of the Communist Party USA, writer Gerald Horne wrote of "a history of the radical, Communist and working-class movement in Hawaii":

It is not well known, I'm afraid, that before statehood in 1959 probably the most vigorous, communist and radical trade union movement under the U.S. flag was in Hawaii.

Investor's Business Daily, August 5, 2008, wrote of Frank Marshall Davis:

Davis was a member of the Moscow-controlled Communist Party USA, according to the 1953 report of the Commission of Subversive Activities of the Territory of Hawaii.

While in Hawaii, Frank Marshall Davis wrote a weekly column, "Frank-ly Speaking," for the labor union paper *Honolulu Record*, headed by the vocal communist, Harry Bridges. (*TIME Magazine*, July 19, 1937.)

In 1956, the House Un-American Activities Committee concluded that the *Honolulu Record* was "a front for the Communist Party," stating:

Mr. Davis' column defends Communists and attacks capitalism with the same vigor as columns appearing regularly in the *Daily Worker* and other frankly Communist publications...

Mr. Davis constantly defended the 11 top United States Communist officials recently convicted in New York on charges of conspiracy to overthrow the Government...

Mr. Davis comments...as follows: "I feel strong sympathy for the Communist minority..."

While in Hawaii, Frank Marshall Davis became friends with Stanley Dunham. *The Telegraph.co.uk*, in the article "Frank Marshall Davis, alleged Communist," August 24, 2008, wrote: "Frank never really did drugs, though he and Stan would smoke pot together."

Stanley Dunham's daughter was Ann Dunham, described as "the original feminist." She married a student from Kenya, Barack Hussein Obama, February 2, 1961. They traveled to Kenya, but Ann was not accepted by his Muslim family. She gave birth to Barack Hussein Obama, Jr. Ann registered his birth in Hawaii, August 4, 1961.

In 1963, Barack Obama, Sr., left Ann to attend Harvard and later wrote an article advocating communism for Kenya. The couple divorced January of 1964 and he died in 1982.

In 1967, Ann Dunham married another student, Lolo Soetoro. Apparently giving up U.S. citizenship, she moved with him to Jakarta, Indonesian where they had a daughter, Maya.

Young Barack Obama returned to Hawaii to live with his grandparents, Stanley and Madelyn Dunham. In 1970, Stanley Dunham introduced his half-white grandson, Barack Obama, to Frank Marshall Davis, whose children were also half-white.

Through his formative years, ages 10 through 18, Barack Obama was friends with Frank Marshall Davis. *The Telegraph.co.uk* wrote in "Frank Marshall Davis, alleged Communist, was early influence on Barack Obama," August 24, 2008:

> Maya Soetoro-Ng, Obama's half-sister, told the Associated Press recently that her grandfather had seen Mr. Davis was "a point of connection, a bridge if you will, to the larger African-American experience for my brother."
>
> In his memoir, Mr. Obama recounts how he visited Mr. Davis on several occasions, apparently at junctures when he was grappling with racial issues, to seek his counsel

Frank Marshall Davis wrote a book, edited by John Edgar Tidwell, *Livin' the Blues* (1992)

Political Affairs writer Gerald Horne wrote:

> At some point in the future, a teacher will add to her syllabus Barack's memoir and instruct her students to read it alongside Frank Marshall Davis' equally affecting memoir 'Livin the Blues.'

Frank Marshall Davis wrote militant poetry on race relations in American culture.

Dr. Rev. Martin Luther King, Jr.
Baptist Pastor
preached nonviolence and
criticized the militant movement.

Davis' writings help fuel the militant Black Muslim movement, Black Nationalist groups and Black Liberation Theology preachers.

Titles of Davis' poems include: Black Man's Verse; I Am the American Negro; Through Sepia Eyes; 47th Street: Poems; Jazz Interludes: Seven Musical Poems; Awakening and Other Poems. Anthologies containing Davis works include: *Livin' the Blues: Memories of a Black Journalist and Poet* (1992); *Black Moods: Collected Poems* (2002); and *Writings of Frank Marshall Davis: A Voice of the Black Press* (2007).

On the other end of the spectrum from the militancy of Frank Marshall Davis was the peaceful nonviolence of Dr. Rev. Martin Luther King, Jr.

Rev. King witnessed the same racial injustice that Davis did, but he responded in a completely different manner.

On April 16, 1963, Rev. King warned from his jail cell in Birmingham, Alabama, of the **dangers of the bitterness and hatred** of Black nationalist groups:

> I must make two honest confessions to you, my Christian and Jewish brothers.
> First, I must confess that over the past few years I have been gravely disappointed with the

white moderate...who is more devoted to "order" than justice....

I began thinking about the fact that **I stand in the middle of two opposing forces in the Negro community.**

One is a force of complacency made up of Negroes who, as a result of long years of oppression, are so completely drained of self-respect and a sense of "somebodiness" that they have adjusted to segregation, and of a few middle-class Negroes who, because of a degree of academic and economic security and because in some ways they profit by segregation, have consciously become insensitive to the problem of the masses.

The other force is one of bitterness and hatred, and it comes perilously close to advocating violence.

It is expressed in the various black nationalist groups that are springing up across the nation, the largest and best-known being Elijah Muhammad's Muslim movement.

Nourished by the Negro's frustration over the continued existence of racial discrimination, this movement is made up of people who have lost faith in America, who have absolutely repudiated Christianity, and who have concluded that the white man is an incorrigible "devil."

I have tried to stand between these two forces, saying that we need emulate neither the "do-nothingism" of the complacent **nor the hatred of the black nationalist.**

For there is the more excellent way of love and non-violent protest.

Rev. Martin Luther King, Jr., continued:

I am grateful to God that, through the **influence of the Negro church, the way of nonviolence became an integral part of our struggle....**

I am further convinced that if our white brothers dismiss as "rabble-rousers" and "outside agitators" **those of us who employ nonviolent direct action** and if they refuse to support our nonviolent efforts, **millions of Negroes will, out of frustration and despair, seek solace and security in black nationalist ideologies - a development that would inevitably lead to a frightening racial nightmare....**

Let me take note of my other major disappointment.

Though there are some notable exceptions, I have also been disappointed with the white church and its leadership.

I do not say this as one of those negative critics who can always find something wrong with the church.

I say this as a minister of the Gospel, who loves the church; who was nurtured in its bosom; who has been sustained by its spiritual blessings **and who will remain true to it as long as the cord of life shall lengthen....**

Rev. Martin Luther King, Jr., concluded:

In the midst of a mighty struggle to rid our nation of racial and economic injustice **I have heard many ministers say, "Those** are **social issues** with which the gospel has no real concern," and **I have watched many churches commit themselves to a completely otherworldly religion** which makes a strange, unbiblical distinction between body and soul, between the sacred and the secular....

I am thankful to God that some noble souls from the ranks of organized religion have broken loose from the paralyzing chains of conformity and joined us as active partners in the struggle for freedom....

Yes, they have gone to jail with us. Some have been kicked out of their churches, have lost the support of their bishops and fellow ministers.

But **they have acted in the faith that right defeated is stronger than evil triumphant.**

Their witness has been the spiritual salt that has preserved the true meaning of the gospel in these troubled times. They have carved a tunnel of hope through the dark mountain of disappointment.

I hope the church as a whole will meet the challenge of this decisive hour...

One day the South will know that when these disinherited children of God sat down at lunch counters they were in reality standing up for what is best in the American dream and for the most sacred values in our Judeo-Christian heritage, thereby bringing our nation back to those great wells of democracy which were dug deep by the founding fathers in their formulation of the Constitution and the Declaration of Independence.

In 1964, Rev. Martin Luther King, Jr. received the Nobel Peace Prize for his biblically inspired writings and actions.

In contrast, Frank Marshall Davis wrote a pornographic autobiography, as reported in *The Telegraph.co.uk*, August 24, 2008:

> It has also been established that Mr. Davis...was the author of a hard-core pornographic autobiography published in San Diego in 1968 by Greenleaf Classics under the pseudonym Bob Greene...
> Mr. Davis confirms that he was the author of *Sex Rebel: Black*...
> The book, which closely tracks Mr. Davis' life in Chicago

and Hawaii and the fact that his first wife was black and his second white, describes in lurid detail a series of shocking sordid sexual encounters.

Barack Obama referred to Frank Marshall Davis several times, mentioning him as "Frank," in his book *Dreams of My Father* (1995).

TIME Magazine's David Von Drehle wrote of Frank Marshall Davis and Barack Obama:

> Davis perceived the Soviet Union as a 'staunch foe of racism' (as he later put it in his memoirs), and at one point he joined the Communist Party...
> It's clear that Obama did seek advice from the old man and that what he got was undiluted.

Newsweek Magazine's Jon Meacham wrote that Barack Obama's mentor, Frank Marshall Davis, who Barack shared alcohol with, was "a strong voice for racial justice...writing on civil-rights and labor issues."

The editor of the Communist Party USA magazine *Political Affairs*, Gerald Horne, claimed that Frank Marshall Davis was a "decisive influence" on Obama.

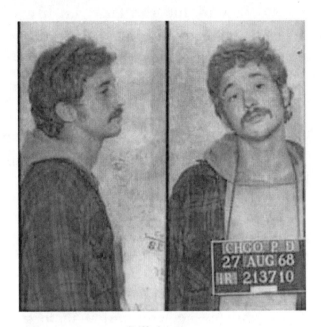

Bill Ayers

Jane Fonda visited Communist North Vietnam
in 1972

BILL AYERS

Another individual with continuing communist connections is Bill Ayers, the son of a Chicago philanthropist and former CEO of the Chicago Edison electric utility company, Thomas Ayers.

In the late 1960's, Bill Ayers helped start the New Left, SDS and the militant group "Weatherman Underground," whose name was inspired by a line in a Bob Dylan song.

On October 6, 1969, Ayers bombed the statue dedicated to the police who died in the 1886 Haymarket Riot. The statue was rebuilt, only to be blown up again by the Weatherman Underground on October 6, 1970.

In 1970, the Federal Government filed charges against Bill Ayers after members of his group died when a nail bomb they were assembling exploded.

In 1970, the Weatherman Underground bombed New York City's Police Headquarters, San Francisco's Police Department and on March 1, 1971, the U.S. Capitol building.

On May 19, 1972, "in retaliation for the U.S. bombing raid in Hanoi," the Weatherman Underground bombed the Pentagon. In July of 1972, Jane Fonda visited Communist North Vietnam.

Bill Ayers

In 1982, FBI assistant director for intelligence, Edward J. O'Malley testified that the Communist Party USA has been:

> One of the most loyal and pro-Soviet Communist Parties in the world and has unfalteringly accepted Soviet direction and funding over the years.

In 1995, Bill Ayers was quoted in the book *Sixties Radicals, Then and Now: Candid Conversations With Those Who Shaped the Era,* by Ron Chepesiuk (Jefferson, NC: McFarland & Co, chapter "Bill Ayers: Radical Educator"):

> I am a radical, Leftist, small "c" communist...Maybe I'm the last communist who is willing to admit it...The ethics of Communism still appeal to me. I don't like Lenin as much as the early Marx.

That same year, 1995, Bill Ayers helped launch Barack Obama's political career by hosting a fund-raiser for him at his home in the Hyde Park neighborhood of Chicago.

Ayers helped start the Chicago Annenberg Challenge, a 501(c)3 education-related nonprofit of which Barack Obama served as the president of the board from 1995 to 2001.

Mark Rudd

From 1999 to 2002, Bill Ayers served with Barack Obama on the board of the Woods Fund of Chicago, a 501(c)3 foundation. The Woods Fund had previously funded Obama's Developing Communities Project, a 501(c)3 foundation, where he was a community organizer from 1985 to 1988.

Bill Ayers donated to Barack Obama's political campaign in 2001.

MARK RUDD

Another continuing communist connection is Mark Rudd. In the article "Another Weatherman terrorist a player in Obama campaign," WorldNetDaily.com, September 27, 2008, Aaron Klein wrote:

> Among the signatories and endorsers to Progressives for Obama is Mark Rudd, one of the main founders of the Weatherman terrorist organization.
>
> Rudd worked closely for years with Weatherman terrorist William Ayers...
>
> In 1968, Rudd traveled with the SDS to Cuba, defying U.S. travel bans, where he says he was heavily influenced by the legacy of Che Guevara and by Cuban-style revolution.

Barack Obama at public campaign
appearance for Raila Odinga

Malik Obama with photo of Barack Obama

RAILA ODINGA

In August 2006, Barack Obama, whose father was of the Luo tribe, made a public campaign appearance for another Luo tribe member, Raila Odinga.

Barack's father had supported Raila Odinga's father, Oginga, even writing a pro-communist article, "Problems Facing Our Socialism," in the *East African Journal,* July 1965, pp. 26-33.) Oginga had been allied with communists and was considered a conduit for communism in Kenya.

Raila Odinga was educated in communist East Germany and lists himself as a social democrat, being supported by many who want to advance Muslim Sharia Law in Kenya.

When Raila Odinga did not win the Presidential Election in Kenya, December 27, 2007, *The Star* reported in an article by Tia Goldenberg, "Dozens burned alive in Kenya," January 2, 2008:

> Some 200 displaced people had sought refuge in the Assemblies of God church in Eidoret, about 300 kilometres northwest of the Kenyan capital

of Nairobi, after their homes were torched in violence following contested elections last Thursday.

Yesterday morning, a mob of about 2,000 people arrived at the church and set it ablaze. Those attempting to flee the inferno were attacked by men wielding machetes...

Kenyan police said more that 70,000 people had been displaced nationwide...

President Mwai Kibaki called for a meeting with his political opponents...but opposition candidate **Raila Odinga** refused, saying he would meet Kibaki only "if he announces that he was not elected."

ACLU'S POT OF GOLD

"It is not fair for taxpayers to pay the legal bills for groups like the ACLU." Currently many towns comply with the demands of the ACLU rather than risk going to trial and paying hundreds of thousands of dollars in legal fees to the ACLU if they lose the case."
- Senator Sam Brownback, 2007

In 1976, Congress passed the Civil Rights Attorney's Fees Awards Act in response to instances of racial discrimination in the workplace, where the offended person had no money to hire an attorney.

This Act was soon co-opted by the ACLU and used to gain profit by suing to remove public displays of faith, then collecting large attorneys' fees.

Los Angeles Seal before ACLU threat (above)
with tiny cross on right.
Redesigned Seal after ACLU (below) with no cross

Phyllis Schlafly wrote in her Eagle Forum newsletter, June 23, 2004:

> **The ACLU is demanding that Los Angeles County remove a tiny cross from its seal...**
>
> The reason **the Los Angeles County Seal** is such a big deal is not because it is a violation of the First Amendment.
>
> It is because a **pot of gold** hiding under it is attracting the ACLU like honey attracts flies.
>
> A little known **1976 federal law called the Civil Rights Attorney's Fees Awards Act enables the ACLU to collect attorney's fees for its suits against crosses, the Pledge of Allegiance, and the Ten Commandments.**
>
> This law was designed to help plaintiffs in civil rights cases, but the ACLU is using it for First Amendment cases, asserting a civil right NOT to see a cross or the Ten Commandments.
>
> The financial lure created by this law is the engine that is driving dozens of similar cases all over the country.

Sam Brownback
U.S. Senator from Kansas

John Hostettler
U.S. Congressman from Indiana

In 2005, Representative John Hostettler-IN helped introduced PERA - Public Expression of Religion Act - to prevent the ACLU 501(c)3 tax-exempt Foundation from receiving attorney's fees for its lawsuits to remove displays of faith.

Rees Lloyd, a former ACLU attorney, is director of the Defense of Veterans Memorials Project of the American Legion Department of California. Rees Lloyd wrote in an article titled "Legion stands up for Scouts after ACLU-DoD settlement," (*The American Legion Magazine*, January 28, 2005):

> The public generally does not know the ACLU is profiting in such cases by millions of dollars in taxpayer-paid "attorney fee awards."...
> Claims by ACLU defenders that the organization once did public good in defending free speech are vitiated by its fanaticism in self-enriching terroristic litigation.

Rees Lloyd, together with the Thomas More Law Center, has helped fight the ACLU 501(c)3 tax-exempt Foundation's lawsuit to remove the cross from the Mt. Soledad.

Mt. Soledad Korean War Memorial
San Diego, California

Mt. Soledad overlooks San Diego, California. It was first used as a Memorial Park in 1914. In 1954, a 29-foot cross was erected to honor Korean War Veterans.

In 1989, two atheists filed a lawsuit to remove the cross. A vote was held and the majority of San Diego citizens wanted the cross to remain. Disregarding the will of the people, Judge Gordon Thompson ordered the cross removed.

In 2006, Supreme Court Justice Anthony Kennedy issued a stay on the lower court's ruling.

In 2006, by a special act of Congress, the Memorial was transferred to the Federal Government as a National Veterans Memorial. Over the several years of this case, the City of San Diego has had to pay thousands of dollars to defend itself.

The American Legion supported the Public Expression of Religious Expression Protection Act. In the article "Legion Lauds Reintroduction of PERA in 110th Congress," it stated:

INDIANAPOLIS (Jan. 31, 2007) - The leader of the nation's largest wartime veterans' organization today applauded Sen.

Rees Lloyd
former ACLU attorney
American Legion Department of California
District 21 Commander

Sam **Brownback** (R-Kan) for reintroducing the **Veterans' Memorials, Boy Scouts, Public Seals and Other Expressions of Religion Protection Act of 2007** (S. 415) in the U.S. Senate, a measure that would **stop the award of taxpayer dollars in legal fees to groups filing lawsuits against veterans' memorials and public displays of religion.**

"Legal attacks against veterans' memorials that display religious symbols **must not be rewarded by judges reaching into taxpayer pockets to enlarge the coffers of organizations such as the ACLU to encourage more lawsuits against our traditions and memorials,**" said American Legion National Commander Paul A. Morin.

The Veterans' Memorials, Boy Scouts, Public Seals and Other Expressions of Religion Protection Act of 2007 would amend U.S. statutes to eliminate the chilling effect on the constitutionally protected expression of religion by state and local officials that results

Judge Roy Moore with
Ten Commandment Monument

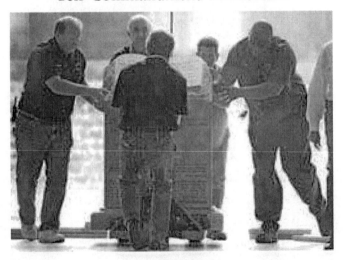

from the threat that potential litigants may seek damages and attorney's fees.

A similar measure passed overwhelmingly in the House last year but the Senate version was not brought up for a vote prior to the adjournment of the 109th Congress.

Most Americans are unaware that activist groups, such as the ACLU, recover hundreds of thousands of dollars from state and local governments each year based on a provision of the 1976 Civil Rights Attorney's Fees Awards Act, which was intended to assist underprivileged plaintiffs in obtaining legal representation in civil rights cases.

Some of these cases include lawsuits against veterans' memorials, the Boy Scouts of America, the public display of the Ten Commandments and other symbols of America's religious heritage.

Last year in a testimony to the Senate, Rees Lloyd, former ACLU attorney and Department of California District 21 Commander, provided these examples of **ACLU awards of taxpayer money**:

Approximately **$950,000 in attorney's fees was awarded to the ACLU in a settlement with the City of San Diego in its lawsuit to drive the Boy Scouts out of Balboa Park.**

In the Judge Roy Moore Ten Commandments case, the ACLU received $500,000.

In a recent "Intelligent Design" case against a school board, the ACLU received $2,000,000 in attorney's fees by order of a judge... These fees were pure profit to the ACLU.

"If the ACLU feels it has to bring lawsuits that most Americans abhor, it should at least have the decency not to assess these to the taxpayers to make a profit," Morin said.

"It is not fair for taxpayers to pay the legal bills for groups like the ACLU," said Brownback.

"Currently many towns comply with the demands of the ACLU rather than risk going to trial and paying hundreds of thousands of dollars in legal fees to the ACLU if they lose the case."

Brownback is a member of the Senate Judiciary Committee and is the ranking member on the Subcommittee on the Constitution, Civil Rights and Property Rights.

"The American Legion will do everything in its power to educate the public about this abusive practice and why this law must be passed," Morin said.

The ACLU 501(c)3 tax-exempt Foundation received:

$150,000 in Georgia from demanding removal of a Ten Commandments display from a courthouse and

$74,462 from demanding a second Ten Commandments display be removed;

$50,000 from demanding a Tennessee Ten Commandments display removed;

$175,000 from demanding an Alabama Ten Commandments display removed; and

$121,500 from demanding a Kentucky Ten Commandments display removed.

Tim Gill
founder of the 501(c)3 Gill Foundation

ACLU'S TAX-EXEMPT FUNDING

"The ACLU is supported by annual dues and contributions from its members, plus grants from private foundations and individuals...

To make a tax-deductible gift to the ACLU Foundation, click here."

\- www.ACLU.org

In 2004, the ACLU 501(c)3 tax-exempt Foundation received over $85 million, mostly from tax-exempt donations from individuals and tax-exempt foundations.

These foundations include: the Rockefeller Foundation, Ford Foundation, Carnegie Foundation, the Playboy Foundation and the Gill Foundation, which was founded by Tim Gill, the QuarkXPress computer software multi-millionaire.

The 501(c)3 Gill Foundation website states its partisan political agenda:

> The Gill Foundation arose out of a battle for equality. A 1992 Colorado ballot initiative denying lesbian and gay men equal protection in the state provoked outrage among fair-minded citizens across Colorado and the nation. One such citizen was Tim Gill...
>
> In just more than ten years of existence, the Gill Foundation has become one of the nation's largest private foundations focused on lesbian, gay bisexual and transgender civil rights.
>
> During these years, the foundation has invested more than $120 million to support programs and nonprofit organizations across the country that share its commitment to equal rights for lesbian, gay, bisexual and transgender Americans

Another 501(c)3 foundation which donates to the ACLU 501(c)3 tax-exempt Foundation is the Tides Foundation, which receives millions from Teresa Heinz Kerry's 501(c)3 Heinz Foundation, and which began the 501(c)4 People for the American Way.

WHY CHURCHES FEAR LOSING TAX-EXEMPT STATUS

"Courts also have never used Thomas Jefferson's celebrated 1802 metaphor about 'a wall of separation between church and state' to stifle churches' support of or opposition to political candidates."

- James D. Davidson, Purdue University

Churches have surrendered their freedom of speech on public issues partly because of a misunderstanding of "separation of church and state," a misunderstanding spread by the ACLU's "legal terrorism" and "terroristic litigation," terms used by American Legion attorney Rees Lloyd (*The American Legion Magazine*, January 28, 2005).

Churches are unaware there are two issues:

1) "Separation of Church and State" - a metaphor describing the First Amendment; and

2) the IRS Tax Code.

"Separation of Church and State" has nothing to do with limiting a church's free exercise of religion, freedom of speech, freedom of press or freedom of assembly.

It is the IRS Tax Code that limits churches, particularly after restrictions were inserted in 1919 and 1934 to limit 501(c)3 educational foundations from spreading Communist propaganda, and especially after the insertion in 1954 of LBJ's Amendment.

Legal scholars question whether the second issue violates the first; whether the IRS Tax laws passed by Congress violate the First Amendments's prohibition that "Congress shall MAKE NO LAW...prohibiting the free exercise" of religion.

IRS Tax laws have intimidated churches, effectively abridging their "freedom of speech," "freedom of the press," and "the right of the people peaceably to assembly," resulting in a number of churches desiring "to petition the Government for a redress of grievances."

Many legal organizations, listed in the appendix of this book, now give free advice to pastors and churches on what specifically they can and cannot do in light of current IRS Tax Code interpretations. In most cases, pastors and churches can do considerably more than what they think.

James D. Davidson of Purdue University summarizes the current situation in his article, "Why Churches Cannot Endorse or Oppose Political Candidates," (see Purdue University *Review of Religious Research*, Vol. 40, No. 1, Sept., 1998, pp. 16-34, Religious Research Association, Inc., www.jstor.org/stable/3512457):

> **The First Amendment** speaks of religious freedom; it says **nothing that would preclude churches from aligning themselves with or against candidates for political office** (Alley, 1988; Hertzke, 1988; 1992; Finke and Stark, 1992).
>
> **The courts also have never used Thomas Jefferson's celebrated 1802 metaphor about "a wall of separation between church and state" to stifle churches' support of or opposition to political candidates** (Padover, 1943:518-519; Bedell, Sandon, and Wellborn, 1982:70-133).

From a constitutional perspective, then, American churches have had every right to endorse or oppose political candidates.

They have not participated in all elections, but they have been actively involved in some...

The reason churches cannot endorse or oppose political candidates is that churches are tax-exempt organizations and must abide by the Internal Revenue Code...

As 501(c)3 organizations, churches must comply with IRS rules...

The ban on electioneering is not rooted in constitutional provisions for separation of church and state.

It actually goes back to 1954 when Congress was revising the tax code, anti-communism was in full bloom, and elections were taking place in Texas.

In this highly-charged political environment, **Lyndon Johnson introduced an amendment banning section 501(c)3 tax-**

exempt organizations from participating in "any political campaign on behalf of any candidate for public office."

His amendment was directed at anti-communist groups such as FACTS FORUM and the Committee for Constitutional Government which stood between him and his goals of crippling McCarthyism, thwarting Allan Shivers' efforts to control the Democratic Party in Texas, and defeating Dudley Dougherty.

Johnson was not trying to address any constitutional issue related to separation of church and state; and he did not offer the amendment because of anything that churches had done.

Churches were not banned from endorsing candidates because they are religious organizations;

They were banned because they have the same tax-exempt status as FACTS FORUM and the Committee for Constitutional Government, the right-wing organizations that Johnson was really after.

LBJ

Charles Grassley
U.S. Senator from Iowa

LBJ LIVES ON

"It is easy to conceive that great evils to our country and its institutions might flow from such a concentration of power in the hands of a few men irresponsible to the people.

Mere precedent is a dangerous source of authority, and should not be regarded as deciding questions of constitutional power."

- President Andrew Jackson, July 10, 1832, Bank Renewal Bill Veto

With the exception of the ACLU 501(c)3 tax-exempt Foundation, Planned Parenthood 501(c)3 tax-exempt Foundation and others, the Federal Government has increased its oversight of religious 501(c)3 tax-exempt organizations since LBJ introduced his Amendment.

This has had a chilling effect on free speech.

As recent as 2007, Senator Charles Grassely decided to investigate six prominent 501(c)3 Christian ministries.

Charles Grassley
U.S. Senator from Iowa

Though the ACLU was against a Senate Committee investigating left-leaning groups during the McCarthy era, the ACLU is silent regarding a Senate Committee investigation of ministries.

This reversal of roles is also seen in Hollywood. During the McCarthy era, actors were "blacklisted" and careers were ended just by an accusation of holding "liberal" communist views.

Today actors are "blacklisted" and careers are ended just by an accusation of holding "conservative" patriotic views.

Just as careers could be ended just by a mere accusation, Christian ministries which are dependent on donations can be ended just by the mere accusation of an investigation.

The dangerous precedent of government oversight of churches and ministries could lead down a slippery slope to conditions which have existed throughout most of world history and still exist in a large parts of the world today, such as in totalitarian China, or under Islamic dhimmi status, or under Mexico's still-in-use 1917 Constitution.

In the article "Senate Probing Top Televangelists for Tax Violations," November 6, 2007, James Joyner wrote:

Letters were sent Monday to the ministries demanding that financial statements and records be turned over to the committee by December 6th.

According to Grassley's office, the Iowa Republican is trying to determine whether or not these ministries are **improperly using their tax-exempt status** as churches to shield lavish lifestyles.

The six ministries identified as being under investigation by the committee are led by: Paula White, Joyce Meyer, Creflo Dollar, Eddie Long, Kenneth Copeland and Benny Hinn. Three of the six - Benny Hinn, Kenneth Copeland and Creflo Dollar - also sit on the Board of Regents for the Oral Roberts University...

A lot of **tax-exempt groups**, religious and otherwise, have long been on the edge in terms of political activism and there have been several investigations, seemingly leading nowhere.

WHO IS LIMITED?

"*T*here is not a shadow of right in the general [federal] government to intermeddle with religion...The subject is, for the honor of America, perfectly free and unshackled. The government has no jurisdiction over it."
- James Madison, June 12, 1788, Journal Entry

In previous chapters, it has been explained that churches' free speech is not limited by "separation of church and state," but rather by the IRS Tax Code.

Nevertheless, the ACLU, has used separation of church and state, "a metaphor based on bad history," to limit individuals, organizations, schools and communities.

It is therefore important to determine if this was what Jefferson intended.

Who exactly did the founders want limited by the First Amendment and the phrase "separation of church and state"?

In his Second Inaugural Address, March 4, 1805, President Thomas Jefferson explained:

> **In matters of religion** I have considered that **its free exercise is placed by the Constitution independent of the powers of the General Government.**
>
> I have therefore undertaken, on no occasion, to prescribe the religious exercise suited to it; but have left them, as the Constitution found them, **under the direction and discipline of state and church authorities by the several religious societies.**

Jefferson's letter to Samuel Miller, January 23, 1808, revealed his understanding that the First Amendment prevented the Federal Government from "inter-meddling with religious institutions":

> I consider **the [federal] government of the United States as interdicted [prohibited] by the Constitution from inter-**

meddling with religious institutions, their doctrines, discipline, or exercises...

This results not only from the provision that no law shall be made respecting the establishment or free exercise of religion, but from that also which reserves to the states the powers not delegated to the United States [10th Amendment].

Certainly no power to prescribe any religious exercise, or to **assume authority in religious discipline, has been delegated to the General government.**

It must then rest with the States as far as it can be in any human authority...

I do not believe it is for the interest of religion to invite the civil magistrate to direct its exercises, its discipline, or its doctrines...

Every religious society has a right to determine for itself the times for these exercises, and the objects proper for them, according to their own particular tenets.

It is obvious that Jefferson's understanding is different than the ACLU's.

Jefferson's view of the First Amendment was not to limit churches, but to limit the Federal or "General" government from interfering or "inter-meddling" in church or State affairs.

Ronald Reagan said in a 1982 Radio Address:

The purpose of that Amendment was to protect religion from the interference of government.

Imagine the dismay if an IRS agent showed up at the Southern Baptist Convention or the American Catholic Bishops' Convention and attempted to "prescribe religious exercises."

Judge Richard Suhrheinrich stated in *ACLU v Mercer County,* 6th Circuit Court of Appeals, December 20, 2005:

The ACLU makes repeated reference to "the separation of church and state."
This extra-constitutional construct has grown tiresome.
The First Amendment does not demand a wall of separation between church and state.
Our nation's history is replete with governmental

acknowledgment and in some case, accommodation of religion.

Associate Justice William Rehnquist wrote in the U.S. Supreme Court case *Wallace v. Jafree*, 1985, dissent, 472 U. S., 38, 99:

> **The "wall of separation between church and state" is a metaphor based on bad history,** a metaphor which has proved useless as a guide to judging.
>
> **It should be frankly and explicitly abandoned.**
>
> It is impossible to build sound constitutional doctrine upon a mistaken understanding of Constitutional history...
>
> The establishment clause had been expressly freighted with Jefferson's misleading metaphor for nearly forty years..
>
> **There is simply no historical foundation for the proposition that the framers intended to build a wall of separation...**
>
> **The recent court decisions are in no way based on either the language or intent of the framers...**

But the greatest injury of the "wall" notion is its mischievous diversion of judges from the actual intentions of the drafters of the Bill of Rights.

U.S. Supreme Court Justice Potter Stewart wrote in *Engle v Vitale*, 1962, dissent:

The Court...is not aided...by the...invocation of metaphors like the "wall of separation," **a phrase nowhere to be found in the Constitution.**

In the U.S. Supreme Court decision, *McCullum v Board of Education*, it stated:

Rule of law should not be drawn from **a figure of speech.**

Justice William O'Douglas wrote in *Zorach v Clausen*, 1952:

The First Amendment, however, does not say that in every and all respects there shall be a separation of Church and State...

We find no constitutional requirement which makes it necessary for government to be hostile to religion and to throw its weight against efforts to widen the effective scope of religious influence...

We cannot read into the Bill of Rights such a philosophy of hostility to religion.

The Supreme Court stated in *Lynch v Donnelly*, 1984:

The Constitution does not "require complete separation of church and state."

Associate Justice William Rehnquist

Potter Stewart
U.S. Supreme Court Justice
nominated by Dwight Eisenhower

RELIGION OF SECULARISM

"Refusal to permit *religious exercises thus is seen, not as the realization of state neutrality, but rather as the establishment of a religion of secularism."*
- Potter Stewart, 1963,
U.S. Supreme Court Justice

Originally, **the First Amendment prohibited the Federal Congress** from having any jurisdiction over the establishment of religion: **"Congress** shall make no law respecting an establishment of religion..."

The word "respecting" meant "concerning." In other words, neither for nor against. It simply was telling the Federal Congress "HANDS OFF," as religion was under each individual State's jurisdiction.

This was stated by Justice Joseph Story.

Joseph Story, Supreme Court Justice
nominated by James Madison

Hugo Black, Supreme Court Justice
nominated by FDR

Justice Joseph Story was nominated to the Supreme Court by James Madison, the person who introduced the First Amendment in the First Session of Congress.

Justice Joseph Story wrote in his *Commentaries on the Constitution,* 1833:

> The whole power over the subject of religion is left exclusively to the State Governments, to be acted upon according to their own sense of justice and the State Constitutions.

Just as **some States allow** consumption of alcohol by minors and **other States do not; some States have** smoking bans and **other States do not; some States allow** gambling and **other States do not,** and s**ome States allow** prostitution (Nevada and Rhode Island) and **the rest do not;** at the time the Constitution was ratified **some States allowed more religious freedom**, such as Rhode Island and Pennsylvania, and **other States**, such as Connecticut and Massachusetts, **did not.**

Congressman James Meacham-VT gave a House Judiciary Committee report, March 27, 1854:

> At the adoption of the Constitution, we believe every State - certainly ten of the thirteen -

provided as regularly for the support
of the Church as for the support of
the Government.

The situation of religion being under
each individual States jurisdiction was
changed as a result of Franklin D. Roosevelt.

FDR was elected President four times,
which led to the 22nd Amendment being passed
to limit future Presidents to only two terms.

During his 12 years in office, Franklin
D. Roosevelt **concentrated** much power in
the hands of the Federal Government.

In 1937, **Franklin D. Roosevelt
nominated Justice Hugo Black to the
Supreme Court.**

Justice Hugo Black **concentrated**
jurisdiction over religion from the States to
the Federal Courts through his 1947 *Everson
v Board of Education* decision.

Whereas the First Amendment
originally limited the Federal Congress, Justice
Black creatively used the 14th Amendment -
which was intended to guarantee rights to
freed slaves - to take jurisdiction over religion
away from each individual "State." He did
this by the insertion of the simple phrase
"Neither a State":

The 'establishment of religion' clause of the First Amendment means at least this: **Neither a State** nor the Federal Government can set up a church.

Neither can pass laws which aid one religion, aid all religions or prefer one religion over another.

Conveniently ignoring innumerable references to and requirements of religion in the various State Constitutions, Justice Black redefined the First Amendment to limit States' jurisdiction over it.

After this, Federal Courts began evolving the definition of "religion" from that of George Mason and James Madison, "Religion...the duty we owe our Creator and the manner of discharging it" (*Virginia Declaration of Rights,* 1776; *Memorial and Remonstrance*, 1785), to a new definition which included "ethical culture," "secularism" and "atheism."

Eventually, so as not to prefer one "religion" over another, Federal Courts prohibited God, which, ironically, established a religion of atheism.

This progression can be seen in several cases. In 1957, the IRS denied tax-exempt status to an "ethical society" stating it did not qualify as a 501(c)3 tax-exempt "church" or "religious society."

The case went to the Supreme Court, where Justice Warren Burger wrote in *Washington Ethical Society v. District of Columbia* (1957):

> We hold on this record and under the controlling statutory language petitioner **[The Washington Ethical Society] qualifies as "a religious corporation or society"**...
>
> It is incumbent upon Congress to utilize **this broad definition of religion** in all its legislative actions bearing on the support or non-support of religion, within the context of the "no-establishment" clause of the First Amendment.

In 1961, Roy Torcaso wanted to be a notary public in Maryland, but did not want to make "a declaration of belief in the existence of God," as required by Maryland's State Constitution, Article 37.

In the Supreme Court case *Torcaso v Watkins* (1961), Justice Hugo Black included a footnote which has been cited authoritatively in subsequent cases:

> **Among religions in this country** which do not teach

what would generally be considered a belief in the existence of God **are** Buddhism, Taoism, **Ethical Culture, Secular Humanism** and others.

Justice Scalia wrote in *Edwards v. Aguillard* (1987):

> In Torcaso v. Watkins, 367 U.S. 488, 495, n. 11 (1961), **we did indeed refer to "SECULAR HUMANISM" as a "religio[n]."**

During the Vietnam War, a Mr. Seeger, who said he could not affirm or deny the existence of a Supreme Being, wanted to be a draft-dodger, claiming to be a conscientious objector under the Universal Military Training and Service Act, Section 6(j), which allowed exemptions for "religious training and belief."

In *United States v Seeger,* (1965), U.S. Supreme Court Justice Tom Clark stated:

> The test of religious belief within the meaning in Section 6(j) is whether it is a sincere and meaningful belief occupying in the life of its possessor a place parallel to that filled by the God of those admittedly qualified for the exemption.

Another draft-dodger case involved Elliot Welsh. The U.S. Supreme Court, in *Welsh v. United States* (1970), decided that belief in a "deity" is not necessary to be "religious":

> Having decided that all religious conscientious objectors were entitled to the exemption, we faced the more serious problem of determining which beliefs were "religious" within the meaning of the statute...
>
> **Determining whether the registrant's beliefs are religious is whether these beliefs play the role of religion and function as a religion in the registrant's life...**
>
> Because his beliefs function as a religion in his life, such an individual is as much entitled to a "religious" conscientious objector exemption under Section 6(j) as is someone who derives his conscientious opposition to the war from traditional religious convictions...
>
> **We think it clear that the beliefs which prompted his objection occupy the same place in his life as the belief in a traditional deity holds in the lives of his friends, the Quakers...**

A registrant's conscientious objection to all war is "religious" within the meaning Section 6(j) if this opposition stems from the registrant's moral, ethical, or religious beliefs about what is right and wrong and these beliefs are held with the strength of traditional religious convictions.

The 7th Circuit Court of Appeals, (W.D. WI) decision in *Kaufman v. McCaughtry,* August 19, 2005, stated:

A religion need not be based on a belief in the existence of a supreme being...**Atheism may be considered...religion...**

'Atheism is indeed a form of religion.' ...The Supreme Court has recognized **atheism as equivalent to a 'religion'** for purposes of the First Amendment...

The Court has adopted a broad definition of **'religion' that includes non-theistic and atheistic beliefs,** as well as theistic ones...

Atheism is Kaufman's religion, and the group that he wanted to start was religious in nature even though it expressly rejects a belief in a supreme being.

Overlooking the detail that the Constitution is only to be changed by Amendments voted in by the majority of the people, the Supreme Court admitted in *Wallace v Jaffree* (472 U.S. 38, 1985) that the original meaning of the First Amendment was modified "in the crucible of litigation," a term not mentioned in the Constitution:

> **At one time it was thought that this right merely proscribed the preference of one Christian sect over another,** but would not require equal respect for the consciences of the infidel, the atheist, or the adherent of a non-Christian faith such as Islam or Judaism.
>
> But when the underlying principle has been examined in the **crucible of litigation**, the Court has unambiguously concluded that the individual freedom of conscience protected by the First Amendment embraces **the right to select any religious faith or none at all.**

It appears the ACLU's use of the phrase "separation of church and state" has resulted in a Federal Government policy favoring, not religious neutrality, but rather the clever establishment of a non-deity based belief system, a state-sponsored atheistic religion.

The ACLU ingeniously used government power to promote a religion of secularism in exactly the way the Constitution rejected.

This was warned against by U.S. Supreme Court Justice Potter Stewart in his dissent in *Abington Township v. Schempp*, 1963:

> **The state may not establish a "religion of secularism"** in the sense of affirmatively opposing or showing hostility to religion, thus "preferring those who believe in no religion over those who do believe"...
>
> Refusal to permit religious exercises thus is seen, not as the realization of state neutrality, but rather as **the establishment of a religion of secularism.**

Ronald Reagan referred to this decision in a radio address, February 25, 1984:

> Former Supreme Court Justice Potter Stewart noted if

religious exercises are held to be impermissible activity in schools, religion is placed at an artificial and state-created disadvantage.

Permission for such exercises for those who want them is necessary if the schools are truly to be neutral in the matter of religion.

And a refusal to permit them is seen not as the realization of state neutrality, but rather as the establishment of a religion of secularism.

U.S. District Court, *Crockett v. Sorenson,* W.D. Va,. 1983:

The *First Amendment* was never intended to insulate our public institutions from any mention of God, the Bible or religion.

When such insulation occurs, **another religion, such as secular humanism, is effectively established.**

Is it just a coincidence that the ACLU's agenda is similar to the Communist agenda read into the Congressional Record, January

10, 1963 by Congressman Albert S. Herlong, Jr., of Florida (Vol 109, 88th Congress, 1st Session, Appendix, pp. A34-A35):

> Eliminate prayer or any phase of religious expression in the schools on the ground that it violates the principle of "separation of church and state."

Ronald Reagan told the Annual Convention of the National Religious Broadcasters, January 30, 1884:

> I was pleased last year to proclaim 1983 the Year of the Bible. But, **you know, a group called the ACLU severely criticized me for doing that. Well, I wear their indictment like a badge of honor.**

At a Fundraiser in Chicago, September 30, 1988, Ronald Reagan stated:

> The **ACLU** often seems to concern themselves with the **rights of criminals** and forget about the **rights of the citizens those criminals prey upon.**

Is the ACLU using the liberties of the First Amendment to take away the liberties of the First Amendment from the majority of the peoples?

Dwight Eisenhower is quoted in the *TIME Magazine* article, "Eisenhower on Communism," October 13, 1952:

> **The Bill of Rights contains no grant of privilege for a group of people to destroy the Bill of Rights.**
> A group - like the **Communist** conspiracy - **dedicated to the ultimate destruction of all civil liberties,** cannot be allowed to claim civil liberties as its privileged sanctuary from which to carry on subversion of the Government.

Ronald Reagan worded it differently on the National Day of Prayer, May 6, 1982

> Well-meaning Americans **in the name of freedom have taken freedom away.** For the sake of religious tolerance, they've forbidden religious practice.

FIRST AMENDMENT

"*T*he First Amendment has been twisted to the point that freedom of religion is in danger of becoming freedom from religion."
- Ronald Reagan, October 13, 1983, Q & A Session

President George W. Bush wrote in his 2003 Proclamation of Religious Freedom Day:

Each year on January 16, we celebrate Religious Freedom Day in commemoration of the passage of the Virginia Statute for Religious Freedom.

The Virginia Statute for Religious Freedom, passed in the Virginia Assembly in 1786, was written by Thomas Jefferson. Jefferson even mentioned it on his tombstone.

Ronald Reagan
40th President
United States of America

In his draft of the Statute, Jefferson wrote:

Almighty God hath created the mind free, and...**all attempts to influence it by temporal punishments...tend only to begat habits of hypocrisy** and meanness, and **are a departure from the plan of the Holy Author of religion,** who **being Lord both of body and mind**, yet chose not to propagate it by coercions on either, **as was in his Almighty power to do,** but to extend it by its influence on reason alone."

George Mason drafted the Virginia Declaration of Rights, which was revised by James Madison, and referred to in his *Memorial and Remonstrance*, 1785:

Religion, or the duty we owe to our CREATOR, and manner of discharging it, can be directed only by reason and conviction, not by force or violence; and, therefore, that **all men are equally entitled to the free exercise of religion,** according to the dictates of conscience, and that **it is the mutual duty of all to practice Christian forbearance,** love and charity toward each other.

On June 7, 1789, James Madison introduced the First Amendment in the first session of Congress with the wording:

> The civil rights of none shall be abridged on account of religious belief or worship.

Justice Joseph Story was appointed to the Supreme Court by James Madison - the man who introduced the First Amendment in the First Session of Congress.

To see the contrast from the original understanding of the First Amendment to the new evolved definition, one need only read Justice Joseph Story's definition in his *Commentaries on the Constitution of the United States*, 1833, Chapter XLIV, "Amendments to the Constitution," Section 991:

> **The real object of the First Amendment** was, not to countenance, much less advance Mohammedanism, or Judaism, or infidelity, by prostrating Christianity; but **to exclude all rivalry among Christian sects.**

Senator Sam Brownback-KS, joined by Senator Tom Coburn-OK, Rep. Walter B. Jones-NC, Rep. Mike Pence-IN, Rep. Joe Pitts-PA, and other members of the 109th Congress supported HR 235, Houses of Worship Free Speech Restoration Act of 2005:

Our founders wrote the First Amendment to protect two vital freedoms: speech about political subjects and religious worship.

On this growing loss of freedom of speech, Ronald Reagan addressed the Alabama State Legislature, March 15, 1982:

To those who cite the **First Amendment** as reason for excluding God...may I just say: The **First Amendment** of the Constitution was not written to protect the people of this country from religious values; **it was written to protect religious values from government tyranny**

In a 1984 Radio Address, Ronald Reagan stated:

Sometimes I can't help but feel the **First Amendment** is being turned on its head...
The **First Amendment** of the Constitution was not written to protect the people from religion; **that**

Amendment was written to protect religion from government tyranny.

In a Q & A Session with the Press, October 13, 1983, Ronald Reagan stated:

The **First Amendment has been twisted** to the point that freedom of religion is in danger of becoming freedom from religion.

In a Radio Address, 1982, Ronald Reagan stated:

Founding Fathers...enshrined the principle of freedom of religion in the **First Amendment...The purpose of that Amendment was to protect religion from the interference of government** and to guarantee, in its own words, "the free exercise of religion."

In a Radio Address, 1982, Ronald Reagan stated:

The **Constitution** was never meant to prevent people from praying; **its declared purpose was to protect their freedom to pray.**

At an Ecumenical Prayer Breakfast, August 23, 1984, Ronald Reagan stated:

The frustrating thing is that those who are attacking religion claim they are doing it in the name of tolerance and freedom and open-mindedness.

Question: **Isn't the real truth that they are intolerant of religion?**

In a Ceremony for Prayer in Schools, September 25, 1982, Ronald Reagan stated:

In the last two decades we've experienced an **onslaught of such twisted logic** that **if Alice were visiting America, she might think she'd never left Wonderland.**

We're told that it somehow violates the rights of others to permit students in school who desire to pray to do so.

Clearly, this infringes on the freedom of those who choose to pray...

To prevent those who believe in God from expressing their faith is an outrage.

"Islam'" means submission and surrender, the
opposite of freedom and liberty.

ACLU & ISLAMIC INTOLERANCE

*"**F**ight those who believe not in Allah...even if they are of the People of the Book, until they pay the jizya with willing submission, and feel themselves subdued."*
- Mohammed, Qur'an, Surah 9:29

Islam is not just a religion. It is also a political system and a military system, because Mohammed was not just a religious leader, he was also a political and military leader.

In strict Islamic countries, Sharia Law limits free speech for non-Muslims, especially those wanting to publicly promote Judeo-Christian beliefs.

In America, the ACLU 501(c)3 tax-exempt Foundation limits free speech for those wanting to publicly promote Judeo-Christian beliefs.

In Islamic countries, Christians and Jews are second class citizens called "dhimmi."

As dhimmi, Christians and Jews are not allowed to practice their faith publicly, pray out loud, ring church bells, spread their beliefs, make converts, show a Cross or Star of David, cannot build new places of worship or repair old ones Muslims destroyed.

Christians and Jews must acknowledge every Muslim as their superior, rising when a Muslim wishes to sit, letting the Muslim pass first on a narrow street, having to feed and house Muslims in their homes, allowing Muslims show disrespect to their places of worship and private meetings, entering whenever they please. Dhimmi cannot own weapons, insult Islam, harbor hostility towards the Islamic government or give aid to those who do.

Islamic Sharia Law relegates individuals holding traditional Judeo-Christian values to an inferior dhimmi status legal position.

Similarly, "hate crime legislation" promoted by the secular left, gay agenda in America, relegates individuals holding traditional Judeo-Christian values to an inferior legal position.

In Islamic countries, Muslims compel Christians, Jews and other infidels, to furnish contributions of money - "jizyah taxes" - for the propagation of Islamic opinions which they disbelieve.

In America, the ACLU favors compelling Christians, Jews and others holding traditional values, to furnish contributions of money - taxes for public schools - for the propagation of atheistic, evolutionist, gay, lesbian, bisexual and transgender opinions in which they disbelieve.

Thomas Jefferson wrote in his *Virginia Statute for Religious Freedom*, adopted January 16, 1786:

> To compel a man to furnish contributions of money for the propagation of opinions which he disbelieves is sinful and tyrannical.

The ACLU 501(c)3 tax-exempt Foundation is effectively establishing a dhimmi status for those in America who hold traditional Judeo-Christian beliefs.

Thomas Jefferson

Harry S Truman
33rd President
United States of America

WILL OF MAJORITY OR MINORITY

"**A**nd of fatal tendency...

to put, in the place of the delegated will of the Nation, the will of a party - often a small but artful and enterprising minority... cunning, ambitious, and unprincipled men will be enabled to subvert the Power of the People and to usurp for themselves the reins of Government."
-   George Washington, September 19, 1796, Farewell Address

The ACLU states on its website:

The power even of a democratic majority must be limited, to ensure individual rights.

This sounds noble until one realizes that for the power of a "democratic majority" to be limited, power must be usurped by an undemocratic minority.

Harry S Truman compared "democracy" with the undemocratic minority rule of "communism" in his Truman Doctrine, March 12, 1947:

> One way of life is based upon the **will of the majority**, and is distinguished by free institutions, representative government, free elections, guarantees of individual liberty, freedom of speech and religion, and freedom from political oppression.
>
> The second way of life is based on **the will of a minority forcibly imposed upon the majority**. It relies upon terror and oppression, a controlled press and radio, fixed elections, and the suppression of personal freedoms.

To prevent the abuse that comes from a concentration of power in "an artful and enterprising minority," America's founders insisted on the rule of law to guarantee power remained with the majority of the people, as the Constitution begins "We the People..."

Calvin Coolidge stated at the ceremony unveiling the Equestrian Statue of Bishop Francis Asbury, October 15, 1924:

The history of government on this earth has been almost entirely **a history of the rule of force held in the hands of a few.**

Under **our Constitution, America committed itself** to the practical application of the rule of reason, with the **power in the hands of the people.**

On June 21, 1788, Alexander Hamilton stated at the New York debates:

The will of the people makes the essential principle of the government.

Jefferson stated (1816, Bergh, Writings, 15:32):

Try...every provision of our Constitution, and see if it hangs directly on **the will of the people.**

James Madison wrote in Philadelphia, January 31, 1792:

The past frequency of wars [is from] a will in the government independent of **the will of the people.**

James Madison wrote in Federalist Paper No. 46, January 29, 1788:

The ultimate authority...resides **in the people** alone.

In 1973, Ronald Reagan stated:

> The **classical Liberal,** during the Revolutionary time, was a man who wanted **less power for the king and more power for the people.**
>
> He wanted **people** to have more say in running of their lives and he wanted protection for the God-given **rights of the people.**
>
> He did not believe those rights were dispensations granted by the king to the people, he believed that he was born with them.
>
> Well, that **today is the Conservative.**

Where America's founders entrusted the preservation of freedom to the will of the majority of the people, the ACLU, knowingly or unknowingly, is wresting power from the will of the people and concentrating it in the hands of a minority of judges.

The ACLU posts on its website: "Majority power is limited by the Constitution's Bill of Rights," yet the Bill of Rights were put in place to limit the Federal Government's power, thereby preserving "majority power."

America's founders feared a repeat of Europe, where power was concentrated in the hands of a king and his appointed judges.

The Declaration of Independence, 1776, stated:

> The history of the present King of Great Britain is a history of repeated injuries and **usurpations**, all having in direct object the establishment of **an absolute tyranny** over these States...
>
> He has made **judges dependent on his will alone...**
>
> A Prince, whose character is thus marked by every act which may define **a Tyrant, is unfit to be a ruler of a free people**.

On June 27, 1936, FDR stated:

> In 1776, we sought freedom from the **tyranny of a political autocracy** - from the 18th century royalists who held special privileges from the crown.
>
> It was to perpetuate their privilege that **they governed without the consent of the governed**; that they denied the right of free assembly and free speech; that they restricted the worship of God.

Colonial Leader John Cotton wrote:

> Whatever...**power** is given will certainly over-run those that give it...

It is necessary therefore, that **all power** that is on earth **be limited.**

In his First Inaugural Address, March 4, 1861, Abraham Lincoln stated:

I do not forget the position assumed by some that constitutional questions are to be decided by the Supreme Court.... **If the policy of the Government** upon vital questions...**is to be irrevocably fixed by decisions of the Supreme Court,** the instant they are made...**the people will have ceased to be their own rulers,** having to that extent practically **resigned their Government into the hands of the eminent tribunal.**

British Statesman Lord Acton wrote to Bishop Mandell Creighton, 1887:

Power tends to corrupt and **absolute power corrupts absolutely**

This is similar to 9th President William Henry Harrison's Inaugural Address, 1841:

The tendency of power to increase itself, particularly when exercised by a single individual... **would terminate in virtual monarchy...**

The danger to all well-established free governments arises from the unwillingness of the people to believe in the existence of designing men...

Like the false Christs whose coming was foretold by the Savior, seeks to, and if it were possible would, impose upon the true and most faithful disciples of liberty...

It behooves the people to be most watchful of those to whom they have intrusted power.

James Madison summed up the dilemma in Federalist Paper #51:

In framing a government which is to be administered by men over men, the great difficulty lies in this: you must first enable the government to control the governed; **and in the next place oblige it to control itself.**

In 1821, Jefferson warned Charles Hammond, almost prophetically, of the temptation for Federal courts to usurp power:

The germ of dissolution of our federal government is in...**the federal judiciary;** an irresponsible body...working like gravity by night and by day, gaining a little today and a little tomorrow, and advancing its noiseless step **like a thief, over the field of jurisdiction, until all shall be usurped from the States, and the government of all be consolidated into one...**

When all government, domestic and foreign, in little as in great things, shall be drawn to Washington as the center of all power, it...will become as... oppressive as the government from which we separated.

Jefferson wrote to William Branch Giles, 1825:

I see...the rapid strides with which the **Federal branch** of our government **is advancing towards the usurpation of all the rights reserved to the States,** and the **consolidation in itself of all powers.**

Jefferson wrote to William Jarvis, September 28, 1820, of despots with absolute, arbitrary power:

You seem...to consider the **judges as the ultimate arbiters of all constitutional questions;** a very dangerous doctrine indeed, and one which would **place us under the despotism of an oligarchy.**

Our judges are as honest as other men, and not more so....and their power [is] the more dangerous, as they are in office for life and not responsible, as the other functionaries are, to the elective control.

The Constitution has erected no such single tribunal, knowing that to whatever hands confided, with corruptions of time and party, its members would become **despots**.

William Henry Harrison stated in his Inaugural Address, March 4, 1841:

Limited are the powers which have been granted, still enough have been granted to constitute **a despotism if concentrated in one of the departments.**

Thomas Jefferson wrote in his Draft Kentucky Resolutions, 1798:

No power over the freedom of religion, freedom of speech, or freedom of the press [was] delegated to the United States by the Constitution...

All lawful powers respecting the same did of right remain and were **reserved to the States or the people.**

Jefferson wrote to Elbridge Gerry, 1799:

I am for preserving to the States the powers not yielded by them to the Union...**I am not for transferring all the powers of the States to the General Government.**

Andrew Jackson said in his Farewell Address, 1837:

It is well known that there have always been **those amongst us who wish to enlarge the powers of the General Government...**

Government would have passed from **the hands of the many** to **the hands of the few.**

Franklin Pierce stated in his Inaugural Address, March 4, 1853:

The dangers of a concentration of all power in the General Government...are too obvious to be disregarded...

The great scheme of our constitutional liberty rests upon **a proper distribution of power** between the State and Federal authorities.

Andrew Jackson vetoed the Bank Renewal Bill, July 10, 1832, stating:

It is easy to conceive that **great evils** to our country and its institutions might flow from such **a concentration of power in the hands of a few men irresponsible to the people.**

Thomas Jefferson wrote to Joseph C. Cabell, 1816:

What has destroyed liberty and the rights of man in every government which has ever existed under the sun? **The generalizing and concentrating all cares and powers into one body.**

Woodrow Wilson stated in New York City, September 4, 1912:

When I resist the **concentration of power,** I am resisting the **process of death,** because **concentration of power is what always precedes the destruction of human initiative.**

Woodrow Wilson addressed the New York Press Club, September 9, 1912:

Liberty has never come from government...The history of liberty is a history of the

limitation of government power, not the increase of it.

Harry S Truman wrote in his *Memoirs - Volume Two: Years of Trial and Hope* (1956):

> The men who wrote the Constitution knew...that **tyrannical government had come about where the powers of government were united in the hands of one man.**
>
> **The system they set up was designed to prevent** a demagogue or "a man on horseback" from **taking over the powers of the government.**
>
> As a young man, I had read **Montesquieu's *Spirit of the Laws*...**
>
> The most important thought expressed in our Constitution is that the **power of government shall always remain limited**, through the separation of powers.

French political philosopher **Montesquieu** wrote in **The Spirit of the Laws**, 1748:

> Constant experience shows us that **every man invested with power is apt to abuse it**...It is necessary from the very nature of things that power should be a check to power.

Secretary of the Navy George Bancroft wrote in *The Progress of Mankind,* 1854:

> **The many** are wiser than **the few;** the multitude than the philosopher.

George Washington stated in his Farewell Address, September 19, 1796:

> **The spirit of encroachment tends to consolidate the powers of all departments in one**, and thus to create, whatever the form of government, a real despotism...
>
> And of fatal tendency... to put, **in the place of the delegated will of the Nation, the will of a party** - often **a small but artful and enterprising minority... cunning, ambitious, and unprincipled men will be enabled to subvert the Power of the People and to usurp for themselves the reins of Government.**

This is no mystery. The Constitution was written by 55 men, but 16 refused to sign it because they thought there were too few limits on the power of the Federal Government.

One who did not sign it was George Mason, called the **"Father of the Bill of Rights."**

Mason was joined by Sam Adams, Patrick Henry and writers of the Anti-Federalist Papers, who insisted **the Bill of Rights be added to the Constitution to prevent power from being taken away from the majority of the people and concentrated in the hands of a minority.**

The ACLU incriminates its own activity of filing lawsuits to remedy perceived injustices when it posts on its website:

> **Majority power is limited** by the Constitution's **Bill of Rights**, which consists of the original **ten amendments ratified in 1791,** plus the **three post-Civil War amendments** (the 13th, 14th and 15th) **and the 19th Amendment** (women's suffrage) adopted in 1920.

Amendments were not to limit "majority power" but "minority power" concentrated in the Government.

In *U.S. v Verdugo-Urquidez* (494 US 247, 288 1990), Justice William J. Brennan, Jr., wrote:

> The term **"the people"** is better understood as a rhetorical counterpoint **"to the government"**...
> The Bill of Rights did not purport to "create" rights.

Rather, they designed the Bill of Rights to **prohibit our government** from infringing rights and liberties presumed to be pre-existing.

The ACLU states: "Majority power is limited by the...Bill of Rights ... the original ten Amendments ... plus ... the 13th ... 14th ... 15th and 19th Amendment[s]," yet **all these Amendments were, in fact, ratified by "majority power."**

U.S. Constitution, 1787, Article V, states:

The Congress, whenever **two thirds of both Houses** shall deem it necessary, shall propose **Amendments** to this Constitution, or, on the Application of the **Legislatures of two thirds of the several States**, shall call a Convention for proposing Amendments, which, in either case, shall be valid to all intents and purposes, as part of this Constitution, **when ratified by the Legislatures of three fourths of the several States.**

"2/3's," "2/3's" and "3/4's" - these are formulas put in place to **keep power** in the hands of majority.

The Constitution and Bill of Rights do not to limit "majority power," they protect it.

If the ACLU wants **to limit power**, it should work through the legislative process to pass laws and Amendments, not file lawsuits.

There are two ways to change laws.

The first way takes time and effort, but it is constitutional. One must persuade a majority of the people to hold particular views, motivate them to vote and elect a majority of the Congressmen and Senators, who in turn, need a majority to pass a law which the President, elected by the majority, signs.

The second way to change laws is quick and easy, and needs only a "minority." Simply find a judge who is willing to change the definitions of words that are in existing laws.

Could it be that the ACLU wants to take power away from the majority because it holds different beliefs than the majority?

A *Gallup Poll* (2007) reported "9 in 10 Americans believe in God"; a *Harris Poll* (2003) reported 90% of Americans believe in God; a *Newsweek* poll (2007) reported 91% of Americans believe in God; and a *Fox News* poll (2004) reported 92% of Americans believe in God.

The Pew Forum's U.S. Religious Landscape Survey (USA Today, February 25, 2008) reported: 80.2 percent of Americans held Judeo-Christian beliefs (51.3% Evangelical/Mainline Protestant; 23.9% Catholic; 1.6% Orthodox & other Christian; 1.7% Mormon; and 1.7% Jewish).

America is obviously less Judeo-Christian than it used to be, but on May 9, 1833, Supreme Court Justice John Marshall wrote to Jasper Adams, President of the College of Charleston, South Carolina:

> **The American population** is entirely Christian, and with us, Christianity and religion are identified.
> It would be strange, indeed, if with such **a people**, our institutions did not presuppose Christianity, and did not often refer to it and exhibit relations with it.

In his Gettysburg Address, November 19, 1863. Lincoln said:

> That we here highly resolve that these dead shall not have died in vain - that this nation, under God, shall have a new birth of freedom - and that government **of the people, by the people, for the people**, shall not perish from the earth.

Walter B. Jones
U.S. Congressman from North Carolina

CONCLUSION

"The ban on *electioneering has nothing to do with the First Amendment or Jeffersonian principles of separation of church and state...*

Just as partisan politics gave birth to the 1954 tax law banning electioneering by tax-exempt organizations, partisan politics also could change it."

    - James D. Davidson, Purdue University, *Review of Religious Research,* September 1998

There is a question as to whether the IRS Tax laws passed by Congress violate the First Amendments's prohibition that "Congress shall MAKE NO LAW...prohibiting the free exercise" of religion

U.S. Representative Walter B. Jones introduced H.R. 2357, the Houses of Worship Political Speech Protection Act, October 1, 2002, stating:

In 1954, then-Senator Lyndon B. Johnson offered an amendment to a revenue bill that would permanently extend the stranglehold of the Internal Revenue Service (IRS) into our nation's churches, synagogues...

Since that time, **the IRS has turned the 501(c)3 code-section on its head** in an attempt to **punish pastors, priests and rabbis for nothing more than communicating the principles of faith during an election period.**

Today we have the chance to **restore the First Amendment rights back to our Nation's pulpits.**

Pastors need to have the freedom **returned to them that Johnson took unfairly 48 years ago.**

More than 2 dozen major national faith based groups and religious leaders believe in this issue, 132 bipartisan Members of Congress believe in this issue, and an overwhelming majority of the American people believe in this issue.

I will continue this fight until...the freedom of speech returns to our houses of worship!

Senator Sam Brownback-KS, joined by Senator Tom Coburn-OK, Rep. Walter B. Jones-NC, Rep. Mike Pence-IN, Rep. Joe Pitts-PA, and members of the 109th Congress joined together in support of HR 235, Houses of Worship Free Speech Restoration Act of 2005:

> **Those who want to silence religious leaders have turned the Constitution on its head.**
>
> This bill will finally lift the fear and anxiety from **houses of worship that seek to speak out on issues that affect the local community and our nation.**

James D. Davidson summarized in his article "Why Churches Cannot Endorse or Oppose Political Candidates," (Purdue University *Review of Religious Research*, Vol. 40, No. 1, Sept., 1998, pp. 16-34, Religious Research Association, Inc., http://www.jstor.org/stable/3512457):

> **The anti-electioneering amendment is grounded in partisan politics** (and not constitutional law)...
>
> **The ban on electioneering has nothing to do with the First**

Amendment or Jeffersonian principles of separation of church and state...

The provision grew out of the **anti-communist frenzy of the 1950s** and was directed at right-wing organizations such as FACTS FORUM and the Committee for Constitutional Government.

It was introduced by Lyndon Johnson as part of his effort to end McCarthyism, protect the loyalist wing of the Texas Democratic Party, and **win reelection to the Senate in 1954...**

Just as partisan politics gave birth to the 1954 tax law banning electioneering by tax-exempt organizations, partisan politics also could change it.

If there were enough support for changing the IRS code - so churches could endorse political candidates without losing their tax-exempt status - the law could be changed.

APPENDIX
HELP & ADVICE

Numerous legal organizations offer advice to pastors, churches and organizations regarding First Amendment questions of what is permissible according to current IRS regulations and potential government abuse of power.

ALLIANCE DEFENSE FUND
15100 N. 90th St.
Scottsdale, AZ 85260
800-TELL-ADF
480-444-0025 fax
www.alliancedefensefund.org

AMERICAN CENTER FOR LAW AND JUSTICE
P.O. Box 90555
Washington, DC 20090
800-296-4529
757-226-2489
757-226-2836 fax
www.aclj.org

BECKET FUND FOR RELIGIOUS LIBERTY
1350 Connecticut Avenue, N.W., Suite 605
Washington, DC 20036
202-955-0095
202-955-0090 fax
www.becketfund.org

CHRISTIAN LAW ASSOCIATION
P.O. Box 4010
Seminole, FL 33775
727-399-8300
727-398-3907 fax
www.christianlaw.org

CHRISTIAN LEGAL SOCIETY
8001 Braddock Rd., Suite 300
Springfield, VA 22151
703-642-1070
703-642-1075 fax
www.clsnet.org

FOUNDATION FOR MORAL LAW
P.O. Box 4086
Montgomery, AL 36103
334-262-1245
334-262-1708 fax
www.morallaw.org

HOME SCHOOL LEGAL DEFENSE ASSOC.
P.O. Box 3000
Purcellville, VA 20134
540-338-5600
540-338-2733 fax
www.hslda.org

JUDICIAL WATCH
501 School St. SW, Suite 500
Washington, DC 20024
888-JW-Ethic
888-593-8442
202-646-5199 fax
www.judicialwatch.org

KLAYMAN LAW FIRM
601 Brickell Key Dr., Suite 404
Miami, FL 33131
305-579-3455
305-579-3454 fax
www.klaymanlaw.com

LANDMARK LEGAL FOUNDATION
19415 Deerfield Ave., Suite 312
Leesburg, VA 20176
703-554-6100
703-554-6119 fax
www.landmarklegal.org

LIBERTY COUNSEL
P.O. Box 540774
Orlando, FL 32854
800-671-1776
407-875-0770 fax
www.lc.org

LIBERTY LEGAL INSTITUTE
903 E. 18th Street, Suite 230
Plano, TX 75074
972-423-3131
972-423-6570 fax
www.libertylegal.org

PACIFIC JUSTICE INSTITUTE
P.O. Box 276600
Sacramento, CA 95827
916-857-6900
916-857-6902 fax
www.pacificjustice.org

RONALD D. RAY, COUNSELORS OF LAW
3317 Halls Hill Farm
Crestwood, KY 40014
502-241-5552
502-241-1552 fax
www.firstprinciplespress.org

THE RUTHERFORD INSTITUTE
P.O. Box 7482
Charlottesville, VA 22906-7482
434-978-3888
434-978-1789 fax
www.rutherford.org

THOMAS MORE LAW CENTER
24 Frank Lloyd Wright Dr.
P.O. Box 393
Ann Arbor, MI 48106
734-827-2001
734-930-7160 fax
www.thomasmore.org

UNITED STATES JUSTICE FOUNDATION
932 D Street Suite 2
Ramona, CA 92065
760-788-6624
760-788-6414 fax
www.usjf.net

Other Resources

AMERICAN MINUTE
P.O. Box 20163
St. Louis, MO 63123
888-USA-WORD
314-487-4395
www.AmericanMinute.com

AMERICAN VISION
P.O. Box 220
Powder Springs, GA 30127
800-628-9460
770-222-7266
770-222-7269 fax
www.AmericanVision.org

EAGLE FORUM
P.O. Box 618
Alton, IL 62002
618-462-5415
618-462-8909 fax
www.EagleForum.org

MAYFLOWER INSTITUTE
P.O. Box 4673
Thousand Oaks, CA 91359
866-566-1620
www.MayflowerInstitute.com

RELIGIOUS FREEDOM COALITION
P.O. Box 77511
Washington, DC 20013
202-543-0300
540-370-4200
www.rfcnet.org

REES LLOYD, ESQ
Defense of Veterans Memorials Project
American Legion Dept. of California
www.reeslloyd.net

RESTORING OUR HERITAGE
1229 Bellemeade Ave.
Evansville, IN 47714
877-500-2USA
812-401-4970
812-401-4971 fax
www.RestoringOurHeritage.com

VISION AMERICA
P.O. Box 10
Lufkin, TX 75902
866-522-5582
936-560-3902 fax
www.visionamerica.us

WALLBUILDERS
P.O. Box 397
Aledo, TX 76008
800-873-2845
817-441-6044
www.WallBuilders.com

PHOTO CREDITS

ACLU http://www.concurringopinions.com/archives/images/ACLU.jpg
Ayers, Bill http://www.edexcellence.net/flypaper/images/20080519ayers.jpg
http://eviltwinbooking.com/media/events/image_7_1.jpg
Baldwin, Roger http://www.constitutioncenter.org/timeline/flash/assets/asset_upload_file83_12161.jpg
http://www.stoptheaclu.com/wp-images/Baldwin.gif
Beecher, Henry Ward http://www.christianchronicler.com/history1/cities_and_d.html
http://userwww.sfsu.edu/~hlcooper/images/HenryWardBeecher.jpg
http://upload.wikimedia.org/wikipedia/commons/d/d2/Henry_Ward_Beecher_-_Brady-Handy.jpg
Berlin Wall http://amhist.ist.unomaha.edu/module_files/Berlin%20Wall.jpg
http://library.thinkquest.org/06aug/02199/Content/Images/berlinWall.jpg
http://www.stmarymagdalenechurch.org/uploads/artwork/Berlin.wall.Reagan.teardown-speech.jpg
Black, Hugo http://upload.wikimedia.org/wikipedia/en/thumb/1/1b/Hugo_Black.jpg/300px-Hugo_Black.jpg
Blues Brothers http://www.worldwardiary.com/history/upload/thumb/2/23/300px-BluesBrothers.jpg
http://www.creativescreenwriting.com/csdaily/csdart/images/2005-08-Aug/Blues%20Brothers%20(225w).jpg
Brownback, Sam http://www.quest-online.com/NewFiles/images/SamBrownback.jpg
Camodian Genocide http://www.icmpa.umd.edu/salzburg/terrorism/wp-content/doc/2007/08/gr4099_khmer3.jpg
http://www.rnw.nl/images/assets/13945033
http://www.historyplace.com/worldhistory/genocide/mass-grave.jpg
http://www.spiegel.de/img/0,1020,343880,00.jpg
http://www.moonbattery.com/cambodia-killing-fields.JPG
Castro, Fidel http://pictures.deadlycomputer.com/d/10927-1/Fidel+Castro1.jpg
Chambers, Whittaker http://media-2.web.britannica.com/eb-media/60/78660-004-F7B14FDF.jpg
Connally, John http://msnbcmedia.msn.com/j/msnbc/Components/Photos/060902/060902_Connally_hmed_3p.h2.jpg
Criswell, W.A. http://www.swordofthelord.com/biographies/CriswellWA.jpg
Davis, Frank Marshall http://www.nathanielturner.com/images/New_Folder/frankmadavis1.jpg
Denton, Jeremiah http://upload.wikimedia.org/wikipedia/en/thumb/a/a4/Jdenton.jpg/160px-Jdenton.jpg
Eagle http://www.azod.com/Conservation%20news/Archive/2004/Articles/flying%20adult%20eagle1.jpg
http://i166.photobucket.com/albums/u93/snow_wolf_31/BaldEagle.jpg
http://www.greenexpander.com/wp-content/uploads/2007/09/gex-bald-eagle.jpg
http://islandfox.org/uploaded_images/beagle-706532.jpg
http://www.alaska-in-pictures.com/data/media/1/perching-bald-eagle_6593.jpg
http://www.birdfinders.co.uk/images/bald-eagle-california-2007.jpg
http://oneyearbibleimages.com/eagle_.jpg
Ebeneezer Baptist Church http://farm4.static.flickr.com/3108/2744613556_be1a2c4673.jpg
Eisenhower, Dwight http://www.medaloffreedom.com/DwightEisenhowerTime1.jpg
http://www.angelismarriti.it/images/EISENHOWER-1945.jpg
http://images.quickblogcast.com/4/9/0/8/2/137097-128094/Dwight_Eisenhower.jpg
http://img.timeinc.net/time/magazine/archive/covers/1945/1101450101_400.jpg
Ellis Island Immigrants http://www.everyculture.com/multi/images/gema_02_img0137.jpg
Finney, Charles http://www.christianchronicler.com/images/Finney.jpg
Fortas, Abe http://www.senate.gov/artandhistory/history/resources/graphic/large/AbeFortas.jpg
Fuller, Melville W. http://upload.wikimedia.org/wikipedia/commons/thumb/9/9d/
Melville_Weston_Fuller_Chief_Justice_1908.jpg/225px-Melville_Weston_Fuller_Chief_Justice_1908.jpg
Field, Stephen J. http://content.cdlib.org/xtf/data/13030/86/ft22900486/figures/ft22900486_00010.jpg
Gannett, Frank http://www2.rit.edu/175/timeline/images/1937.Gannett_thumb.jpg
Gill, Tim http://img.timeinc.net/time/daily/2007/0704/gill_tim0404.jpg
http://www.gillfoundation.org/img/glf/logo_print.gif
http://www.familydiv.org/images/fund_gill.gif
Grassley, Charles http://cache.daylife.com/imageserve/059B8XW2to1ZQ/610x.jpg
http://media.npr.org/programs/morning/features/2007/nov/grassley/grassley200.jpg

http://www.nytimes.com/2007/09/27/business/27letter.html?_r=1&oref=slogin
Hand, Judge Learned http://www.allianceadv.com/images/learned_hand_owwc.jpg
Hays, Wayne http://cha.house.gov/images/stories/hays.jpg
Hiss, Alger http://upload.wikimedia.org/wikipedia/commons/3/31/Mugs(14).jpg
Ho Chi Minh http://www.notablebiographies.com/images/uewb_05_img0344.jpg
http://www.dictatorofthemonth.com/Ho/ho1.jpg
Hunt, H.L. http://www.jfk-fr.com/images/bio/169.jpg
Johnson, Lyndon Baines http://www.visitingdc.com/images/lyndon-johnson-picture.jpg
http://z.about.com/d/americanhistory/1/0/0/A/36_lbj_1.jpg
http://www.wellesley.edu/Polisci/wj/Vietimages/Audio/0,1020,249029,00.jpg
http://msnbcmedia3.msn.com/j/msnbc/Components/Photos/070119/070119_LBJ_vmed_2p.widec.jpg
http://www.archives.gov/press/press-kits/picturing-the-century-photos/images/lbj-and-richard-russell.jpg
http://drx.typepad.com/psychotherapyblog/images/2007/07/26/lbj_2.jpg
http://upload.wikimedia.org/wikipedia/commons/c/c3/37_Lyndon_Johnson_3x4.jpg
http://academic.brooklyn.cuny.edu/history/johnson/lbj-phone.bmp
http://cache.daylife.com/imageserve/0emEgpxgGk5kq/610x.jpg
http://images.chron.com/blogs/txpotomac/LBJ%20in%20San%20Marcos.jpg
http://drx.typepad.com/psychotherapyblog/images/2007/08/03/lbj_and_kennedy.jpg
http://www.lbjlib.utexas.edu/johnson/museum.hom/museum_exhibit_images/timeline/EPILOG.JPG
http://content.answers.com/main/content/wp/en/thumb/0/09/250px-FDR-LBJ.png
Hoover, Herbert http://www.nps.gov/heho/historyculture/images/herbet_hoover_415w.jpg
http://www.coverbrowser.com/image/time/877-1.jpg
Hostettler, John http://wwwimage.cbsnews.com/images/2005/06/21/image703201x.jpg
Hungary invasion http://socialistworld.net/pics/p295_03.jpg
http://www.filolog.com/images/budapest_56_04.jpg
http://www.filolog.com/images/budapest_56_04.jpg
Islam http://www.zionism-israel.com/ezine/Isllam1.jpg
http://x03.xanga.com/2f4a62f4c263271918311/b48399968.jpg
http://www.sondrak.com/archive/Nick%20Berg%20Beheading%20Pic%203%20-%20WARNING%20GRAPHIC!!%20(2).jpg
Jefferson, Thomas http://richmondthenandnow.com/Images/Famous-Visitors/Thomas-Jefferson-big.jpg
Jones, Walter B. http://upload.wikimedia.org/wikipedia/commons/9/9c/
Walter_B._Jones,_official_Congressional_photo.jpg
Kennedy, John F. http://www.bet.com/Assets/BET/Published/image/jpeg/4e3dc986-49d5-0e5d-a2a3-d304c107d942-
news_fb_JohnFKennedy.jpg
Kenya, Reuters
King, Jr., Martin Luther http://upload.wikimedia.org/wikipedia/commons/8/84/Martin_Luther_King_Jr_NYWTS.jpg
http://www.lib.fit.edu/pubs/librarydisplays/BlackHistory/494px-Martin_Luther_King_Jr_NYWTS.jpg
http://www.uweb.ucsb.edu/~syork/MartinLutherKingQuotes.jpg
KKK http://www.martinfrost.ws/htmlfiles/kkk_dcmarch.jpg
Leland, John http://elbourne.org/images/leland.jpg
Lloyd, Rees http://www.reeslloyd.net/Rees_Lloyd.JPG
Los Angeles County Seal http://ladpw.org/PDD/Beach_Bus/LACoSEAL.jpg
http://www.allstates-flag.com/fotw/images/u/us)calac.gif
Mattachine Review http://sitemaker.umich.edu/lesbian.history/files/mattachine_review_1959.jpg
Mao Zedong http://incontiguousbrick.files.wordpress.com/2007/06/mao-zedong-3.jpg
McCarthy, Joseph http://upload.wikimedia.org/wikipedia/commons/f/fa/Joseph_McCarthy.jpg
Mindszenty, Cardinal Joseph http://www.osaarchivum.org/files/holdings/selection/rip/4/pc/300-40-5—124-2-1_000052.jpg
http://www.tldm.org/News4/Mindszenty_Time.jpg
Mitrokhin, Vasili http://news.bbc.co.uk/olmedia/445000/images/_446111_mitrokhin150.jpg
Moody, Dwight L. http://www.wholesomewords.org/images/moodyr.jpg
Moore, Judge Roy http://www.sonstoglory.com/images/JudgeRoyMooreTenCommandmentsRemoval.jpg
http://www.wvbmh.com/images/Moore_TenC.gif
Nazi Skokie, Illinois http://www.law.umkc.edu/faculty/projects/ftrials/conlaw/fcolin.jpg

http://www.skokie.lib.il.us/s_info/in_biography/attempted_march/collins.jpg
Obama, Malik http://pal2pal.com/BLOGEE/images/uploads/obamamuslimdress.jpg
Odinga, Raila http://atlasshrugs2000.typepad.com/atlas_shrugs/images/2008/01/11/obama_odinga.jpg
Pot, Pol http://www.historyplace.com/worldhistory/genocide/pol-pot2.jpg
Reagan, Ronald http://www.science.co.il/People/Ronald-Reagan/images/Ronald-Reagan-1985.jpg
Rehnquist, William http://upload.wikimedia.org/wikipedia/commons/3/31/William_Rehnquist.jpg
Roosevelt, Franklin D. http://media-2.web.britannica.com/eb-media/19/78319-004-545F8CDD.jpg
Rudd, Mark http://www.mugshots.com/IMAGES/P__Mark-Rudd.jpg
Smith, Al http://www.kevincmurphy.com/alsmith.jpg
http://www.explorepahistory.com/images/ExplorePAHistory-a0k7h7-a_349.jpg
Stalin, Joseph http://www.historywiz.com/images/coldwar/stalin3.gif
Stevenson, Coke http://www.tsl.state.tx.us/governors/personality/stevenson-p01.jpg
Steward, Potter http://upload.wikimedia.org/wikipedia/commons/a/ae/US_Supreme_Court_Justice_Potter_Stewart_-_1976_official_portrait.jpg
Story, Joseph http://www.nndb.com/people/495/000050345/joseph-story.jpg
Sunday, Billy http://ameshistoricalsociety.org/exhibits/residents/billy_sunday_pose1.jpg
Truman, Harry S http://www.sos.mo.gov/archives/exhibits/TrumanProject/images/Truman.jpg
http://vwt.d2g.com:8081/truman_t1_1943_investigator.jpg
U.S. Treasury Building http://upload.wikimedia.org/wikipedia/commons/0/05/US-Treasury-Large.jpg
Washington, George http://www.artinthepicture.com/artists/Gilbert_Stuart/george_washington.jpeg
Whitfield, George http://www.umich.edu/~ece/student_projects/slavery2/georgewhitfield.jpg
http://richardperkins.blogsome.com/images/thumb-whitfield.jpg
http://www.2112.net/cheeze/img/blog/whitfield.jpg
Wilson, Wilson http://upload.wikimedia.org/wikipedia/commons/thumb/2/2d/
President_Woodrow_Wilson_portrait_December_2_1912.jpg/492px-
President_Woodrow_Wilson_portrait_December_2_1912.jpg

ACLU, IRS & LBJ THREATEN EXTINCTION OF FREE SPEECH   243

CPSIA information can be obtained
at www.ICGtesting.com
Printed in the USA
FFOW02n0000101117
43384469-41977FF